Louis D. Brandeis
and the
Progressive Tradition

Melvin I. Urofsky

Louis D. Brandeis

and the

Progressive Tradition

Edited by Oscar Handlin

Little, Brown and Company · *Boston* · *Toronto*

for Sharyn

LIBRARY OF CONGRESS CATALOG CARD NO. 80-81814

ISBN 0-673-39354-2

I H G F E D C B

HAL

PRINTED IN THE UNITED STATES OF AMERICA

Editor's Preface

THE SEVERAL careers of Louis D. Brandeis spanned a perilous transition in the life of the American people. In the years between his birth and his death a rural society became urban. Industry displaced agriculture as the basis of the country's wealth. A massive wage labor force in manufacturing differed in character and in ethnic origin from the farmers and artisans who had earlier composed the bulk of the population. The effects of these developments rippled outward to reorient municipal, state, and national politics, and in a way of which few were conscious transformed the practice of law.

The social, economic, and political issues raised by these changes troubled many citizens. But men and women accustomed to growth as a constant of their history did not surrender their traditional optimism. A firm belief in progress persuaded them that humanity was capable of indefinite improvement, and a variety of movements took form to achieve that end. After 1900, they became known collectively as progressives. Although the progressives never formed a homogeneous party subscribing to a uniform platform, they shared intellectual features. They insisted that policy had to rest on knowledge and on the use of rational methods, and they regarded efficiency as a goal that would maximize benefits to the whole population. The evolving ideas of Louis D. Brandeis revealed how important those assumptions were.

Brandeis began his career as an attorney, but learned the extent to which the law became involved in social change. His dawning awareness of the new problems made him an adviser to President Wilson and in time carried him to the bench of the United States Supreme Court. Late in life also he discovered his identity as a Jew, and that led him to confront the issue of ethnicity in the modern world. The complex story unfolded in Professor Urofsky's book thus illustrates the main lines in the evolution of the American progressive movement.

OSCAR HANDLIN

Contents

I

Beginnings

LOUIS DEMBITZ BRANDEIS's life spanned nearly a century of this country's history. Born in Louisville, Kentucky, four years before the Civil War, on November 13, 1856, he died on the eve of World War II, on October 5, 1941. During his eighty-five years the United States grew from a provincial agrarian country into a mighty industrialized giant with global interests and responsibilities. Through Civil War and Reconstruction, through Greenbacker and Populist and Progressive unrest, through Square Deal and New Freedom and New Deal, through boom and bust, Brandeis clung to a belief in essential, immutable values. Despite the dizzying pace of change, his vision of what constituted a good society remained intact. He was not blind to events and developments in the world nor afraid of change per se. The quality of life, its opportunities, its challenges, its moral tone, mattered greatly to him, and he spent his talents and energy attempting to preserve the democratic, open nature of the society he knew and cherished as a youth.

Louisville in the 1850s and 1860s was hardly a frontier society, nor were the Brandeises pioneering in an uncharted wilderness. The city's strategic position on the Ohio River made it a natural center for the region's commerce, a situation that had drawn Adolph and Frederika Brandeis there after their emigration from Bohemia in the wake of the 1848 revolutions. Although not involved in the political struggle, the Brandeis family had been touched by the liberals' vision;

they and a number of their relatives decided to seek a freer life in the New World. Reasonably well educated and cultured, they soon prospered as Adolph's grain business expanded in the boom years of war and reconstruction. They also played an active role in the German-speaking community, which was attempting to re-create the literary and artistic life many had known in the old country. Musicales, debating societies, literary clubs, good talk and plenty of it were part of the milieu in which young Louis grew up.

Equally important to the family was a basic and deep-felt love of America and a commitment to democracy. Although the Brandeises cherished much about Europe and its culture, they remembered its political despotism as well. Young Louis received a taste of this at first hand when his father, anticipating the depression of 1873, closed his business and took the family on an extended visit back to Europe. There Brandeis enrolled in the Annen-Realschule in Dresden. His grades during the two years he attended the school were excellent, and he won a prize in 1875 "for industry and good behavior." Moreover, the academic rigor of the German school taught him how to think methodically, how to use experience and knowledge to develop new ideas. But the strict paternalism and authoritarian rules repelled him. One evening he returned late to find himself locked out, and he had to whistle to awaken his roommate in order to open the door. For this offense the headmaster severely reprimanded him. The experience left the young democrat homesick. "In Kentucky you could whistle! I wanted to go back to America." In the spring of 1875 he got his wish, and the family returned to begin rebuilding its fortunes. That fall Louis Brandeis entered the Harvard Law School.

The study of law was then in transition. Instead of reading in a lawyer's office, a form of apprenticeship, more and more young men were enrolling in law schools. At Harvard Christopher Columbus Langdell spearheaded a major revolution in legal training with the case method of study. Langdell believed that essential legal doctrines could best be understood through a rigorous examination of the cases in which they had developed. Although some lawyers and teachers looked askance at the new pedagogy, Brandeis embraced it enthusiastically. "When the end of the chapter of cases is reached, the student stands possessed of the principles in their full development. Having attended as it were at their birth, having traced their history from stage to stage, the student has grown with them and in them. . . . Once acquired, they cannot be forgotten; for they are a part of himself."

The years at Harvard were happy; Louis excelled in his studies, and his love of the law deepened. To his cousin Otto Wehle he wrote: "You have undoubtedly heard from others of my work here, how well I am pleased with everything that pertains to the law, yet my own inclination would prompt me to repeat the same to you, though at the risk of great reiteration. My thoughts are almost entirely occupied by the law. . . . Law schools are splendid institutions." About the only difficulty Brandeis faced involved recurrent eye problems, and he feared for a while that he might have to give up his cherished dream of becoming a lawyer. Ultimately a noted New York doctor found nothing wrong other than severe strain induced by long hours of reading in the flickering light of a gas lamp and advised that "it won't hurt you to read less and think more." As a result Brandeis worked hard to develop his already impressive retentive powers. In later years he would amaze both friend and foe with his phenomenal memory, which seemingly retained everything he had ever learned about a case or an issue.

In his two years of regular study as well as a year of postgraduate work, Brandeis compiled a nearly perfect academic record, impressing all whom he met with his knowledge of the law as well as his ability to think logically. After graduation his parents wanted him to settle in Louisville, but his favorite sister Fanny and her husband Charles Nagel persuaded him to join them in St. Louis. His year of practice there, however, proved unrewarding, and he found the intellectual climate of the city dull after the excitement of Cambridge. When a classmate, Samuel D. Warren, proposed a partnership in Boston, the young Brandeis jumped at the opportunity. In July 1879 the firm of Warren & Brandeis opened its doors at 60 Devonshire Street.

The firm prospered almost at once. Warren's extensive social connections, as well as his family's paper business, attracted clients, and the abilities of the two attorneys held them. Former teachers at the law school also sent business their way, and firms from outside the Boston area began contracting with the office to represent their clients in local matters. Brandeis's legal abilities, both in written briefs and in oral presentations, were soon widely acknowledged. Chief Justice Horace Gray of the Supreme Judicial Court of Massachusetts, for whom Brandeis also served as a clerk, considered him "the most ingenious and most original lawyer I ever met, and he and his partner are among the most promising law firms we have got."

Brandeis was to remember these early years in Boston as the happiest of times. His own native brilliance as well as his friendship with Warren won him easy entry into the city's social life. The late nineteenth century marked a high point in the cultural and literary life of Boston, and Brandeis's hours away from the office found him associating with the Emertons, Thayers, Delands and others whose salons were the gathering points of Brahmin intellectuals. One of his earliest friendships was with Oliver Wendell Holmes, Jr., and he frequently took supper with Holmes and his wife at the Parker House. Brandeis, in fact, arranged the endowed chair that brought Holmes for a brief period to the Harvard Law School.

But Brandeis did more than just hobnob with Boston's finest; he imbibed an entire set of values and traditions, making them his own to the point where his law partner characterized him as "more Brahmin than the Brahmins." In the 1870s and 1880s Boston still valued the reform heritage passed down from its Puritan founders. Massachusetts had been in the forefront of the antislavery movement, had pioneered in child labor and factory laws, and in general had accepted the need for a society to protect its less fortunate, more vulnerable members; it acknowledged as a constant social value the need to improve. This impulse for reform had not come from the bottom but from the top, from an elite that took its social responsibilities seriously.

The Boston tradition included strong emphasis on self-reliance in a competitive economic environment. Granted, the weak had to be protected against predators; but success and its rewards went to those who fought for and earned them. Brandeis was no egalitarian; he did not believe in a society that reduced all people to a single level. Human beings had to strive, but they had to do so fairly, and despite the struggle they had civic obligations to fulfill. The role of citizen, with all the privileges and responsibilities the word entailed, was in Brandeis's eyes the most important a person could fill.

Ironically, Louis Brandeis's devotion to the older political tradition — with its emphasis on honesty and civic responsibility, its adherence to open and unfettered competition, even its insularity and provincialism — would bring down upon his head the wrath of those Brahmin leaders who had succumbed to the temptations of the new finance capitalism. Many State Street stalwarts would one day be embarrassed when this outsider publicly called upon them to adhere to their tradition of high ethical standards.

At the same time that he and Warren were building up their practice, Brandeis also gave serious thought to teaching. "I recognize that when the time comes," he wrote, "I shall have to decide between [teaching] and practice. . . . The law as a logical science has very great attractions for me. I see it now again by the almost ridiculous pleasure which the discovery or invention of a legal theory gives me; and I know that such a study of the law cannot be pursued by a successful practitioner."

In March 1882 the opportunity presented itself in an offer from Harvard President Charles Eliot to teach a course in evidence the following year. Brandeis accepted with alacrity, much to the joy of his family. He proved an excellent teacher, and the law faculty offered him an assistant professorship. Despite the urgings of his parents, however, Brandeis opted for the combat of the courtroom. As he wrote to his brother: "I really long for the excitement of the contest, that is, a good prolonged one covering days or weeks. There is a certain joy in the draining exhaustion and backache of a long trial, which shorter skirmishes cannot afford." No one, especially Louis Brandeis, recognized at this time that his career as a legal educator in the broadest sense was at its beginning, not its end.

With the decision now firmly made, Brandeis threw himself into practice wholeheartedly, and the growth of Warren & Brandeis into one of the largest offices in New England was due primarily to his drive, ambition, and ability (Warren withdrew from the partnership in 1889 upon the death of his father in order to take over management of the family's paper mills). The practice was extensive, and Edward J. McClennen, who later became a partner in the firm, recalled that Brandeis at one time or another handled every kind of litigation, including some criminal cases. The Brandeis technique involved not only thorough knowledge of the law but complete mastery of the facts involved in the case. In a notebook he wrote: "Know thoroughly each fact. Don't believe client witness. Examine documents. Reason. Use imagination. . . . Far more likely to impress clients by knowledge of facts than by knowledge of law. Know not only specific case, but the whole subject. Can't otherwise know the facts. Know not only those facts which bear on direct controversy, but know all the facts and laws that surround."

Brandeis's ability to master "all the facts and laws that surround" proved to be the key to his success, for the relationship between lawyers and their business clients was then passing through a critical transformation. Previously when a businessman had gone to see a lawyer, litigation had already been decided upon; for an action that had been initiated or completed, the client was either suing or needed defense against a suit. The lawyer acted on behalf of his client after the fact. The widespread adaptation of the corporate form, the increase of multistate and multiparty transactions, the establishment of state and federal regulations, and the growing complexity of an industrial economy made that procedure increasingly costly, not only in legal fees but in tied-up resources and delays. Gradually businessmen began to seek out lawyers before reaching decisions or initiating expensive plans. Now they needed advice and guidance on what to do to avoid legal problems. "A lawyer's chief business," said Elihu Root, "is to keep his clients out of litigation."

But to serve effectively as counsel to businessmen and corporate clients, a lawyer had to know, as Brandeis had already perceived, not only the law but the facts of the situation as well. He had to know as much about his client's business as his client did, for his advice not only touched on legal matters but affected financial decisions as well. In a letter to one of the junior members of the firm, Brandeis set out his philosophy regarding this new role of counsel: "Knowledge of the decided cases and of the rules of logic cannot alone make a great lawyer. He must know, must feel 'in his bones' the facts to which they apply — must know, too, that if they do not stand the test of such application the logical result will somehow or other be avoided. . . . When from a knowledge of the law, you pass to its application, the need of a full knowledge of men and of their affairs becomes even more apparent. The duty of a lawyer today is not that of a solver of legal conundrums; he is indeed a counselor at law. . . . Your law may be perfect, your ability to apply it great and yet you cannot be a successful advisor unless your advice is followed; it will not be followed unless you can satisfy your clients, unless you impress them with your superior knowledge and that you cannot do unless you know their affairs better than they because you see them from a fullness of knowledge."

Brandeis practiced what he preached. He impressed his

clients not only with his legal abilities but with his comprehensive understanding of the business world and of their affairs. His conduct of his own practice also left little doubt in clients' minds as to his businesslike approach. His office was spartanly furnished, and in the winter the temperature was set so low that visitors had to keep on their overcoats. One did not chat at leisure with Louis Brandeis; one presented the problem, and Brandeis probed the matter, frequently getting to the heart of a seemingly complicated issue in a matter of moments. Then the client could escape to a more hospitable clime while Brandeis and his associates followed up with research, analysis, and if necessary, litigation.

Perhaps the best-known example of Brandeis's work as counsel occurred when William H. McElwain sought advice on labor problems in his large shoe manufacturing company. Times were not so good, McElwain explained, and he wanted his workers to accept a pay cut; when business conditions had been better, he had paid a very high wage, and now an adjustment was in order. By steady questioning, however, Brandeis soon found out that nearly every worker, through no fault of his own, suffered long layoffs during slack periods. The high wages for days worked when combined with the absence of income during enforced idleness yielded a miserably low annual wage.

To remedy this situation, Brandeis suggested that McElwain reorganize his business, putting it on a more rational basis by securing his orders well in advance. He could then run his factory on a regular schedule, spacing orders to fill in previously slack times. The workers could thereby accept a cut in hourly rates because they would be working many more days during the year, thus earning a higher annual income. McElwain accepted the advice, to the benefit of his employees as well as his stockholders. Brandeis's contribution lay, as he had written to Dunbar, in learning more about the shoe business than the manufacturer had and then being able to put together a plan that resolved the problem without resorting either to a confrontation with the workers or litigation.

The method worked. Filene Department Store, Carter Ink Company, McElwain Shoe Manufacturers, and other major firms sought out his services and paid handsomely for them. In 1890 when three-fourths of the country's attorneys made less than $5,000 annually, Brandeis earned over $50,000. By 1907 he had made his first million, and he would have his second before he moved to the United States Supreme Court in 1916.

From nearly the day he and Sam Warren had opened their doors, they had kept busy, and the success of the firm led to its enlargement and later, under Brandeis's management, to a substantial reorganization. Each year Warren & Brandeis brought in a few top graduates of the Harvard Law School to work in the office. Some stayed only a year or two to learn their trade and then opened their own successful practices. Others, like William H. Dunbar, George R. Nutter, and Edward F. McClennen, stayed on, ultimately becoming partners. As the office and its business expanded, Brandeis began to delegate much of the work to subordinates. He took younger men, gave them exceptional opportunities, and credited them for their efforts. But the firm in many ways resembled the other large law factories of the time, and Brandeis, who later would become an arch foe of bigness, staunchly defended the size and organization of his own firm, arguing that large offices allowed each man to find his own strength and to specialize in the areas he could handle best.

During this active period as an attorney, Brandeis developed a life-style that would characterize the rest of his years. As a youth he had been physically weak, and all his life he attempted to sustain his health by regular exercise. He rode frequently, but his favorite activity was canoeing, in which he excelled. He also learned to pace himself, and he took time off for a vacation, no matter how brief, whenever he felt that his intellectual outlook was dulled. "A bookkeeper can work eight or ten hours a day and perhaps twelve, year in and year out, and possibly his work may always be good (tho' I doubt it). But a man who practices law, who aspires to the higher places of his profession, must keep his mind fresh. . . . The bow must be strung and unstrung." Eventually Brandeis developed the pattern of taking off the entire month of August. "I soon learned," he later said, "that I could do twelve months' work in eleven months, but not in twelve." In August Brandeis left work to hike in the wilderness, to sail and canoe, and to catch up on his reading.

After 1891 his vacation time was spent with a family. Long a bachelor, Louis at last succumbed to the charms of his cousin, Alice Goldmark. In her he found a devotion to high moral principles and a love of literature and culture to match his own. They had two daughters, Susan and Elizabeth, and in their home they re-created the close-knit warmth and unity each had known in their youth. With his large income the Brandeis family could have lived extremely comfortably, affording a large house, several servants, and many luxuries. But in the words of Matthew Arnold, which both knew and cherished, "Life is not a having and a getting, but a being and a becoming." Louis and Alice Brandeis resolved to be free. By this they meant not only freedom from financial straits but freedom to do the things that really mattered to them, to have the time, the resources, and the independence to work as they chose, for the causes in which they truly believed. So they lived simply, almost frugally. His income easily paid for the necessities, and the bulk of it he put away in extremely conservative investments.

The lure of get-rich-quick schemes in the stock market never held any appeal for him, and he lectured his brother on the danger of speculation: "I feel very sure that people like us ought not to buy and sell stocks. We don't know much about the business — and beware of people who think they do. Prices of stocks are made, they don't grow; and their fluctuations are not due to natural causes. . . . My idea is that your situation is about like mine — namely to treat investments as a necessary Evil — indulging in the operation as rarely as possible. Buy only the thing you consider very good, and stick to it unless you have cause to doubt the wisdom of the purchase.

And when you buy, buy the thing which you think is safe, and will give you a fair return, but don't try to make your money out of investments. Make it out of your business. . . . Take in that all the risks you think it prudent to take — but risk only there."

Brandeis's later disenchantment with investment bankers, his scorn of those who lost money in stock operations, dated back to these beginnings. As in other areas, here too he adhered rigidly to his own advice. Aside from token purchases of stock in his clients' companies, a necessary gesture in order for him to participate legitimately in stockholder meetings, he limited his investments almost entirely to railroad, utility, and government bonds. Even the ownership of real property interested him hardly at all. For years he rented summer homes on Cape Cod, and he bought a house in Chatham when that became the only way he could ensure his continued privacy there.

Privacy was one of the things that mattered to him, and when that of Sam Warren was invaded by tabloid newspapers, he wished to help his friend. After Warren married Mabel Bayard, the young couple entertained extensively, and the *Saturday Evening Gazette* reported the events in lurid detail. Annoyed by the unwanted publicity, Warren and Brandeis, although no longer in partnership, researched the law on privacy. Although they found no legal remedy, they did write an article that scholars later considered the foundation for the development of the doctrine of privacy. Here again the early beginnings were not forgotten; devotion to the "right to be left alone" received eloquent restatement years later when as Mr. Justice Brandeis he vigorously protested the government's use of wiretaps in a dissenting opinion in *Olmstead* v. *U.S.*

Other things mattered as well. He saw himself as a lawyer, a man engaged in a profession, who stood in a position of parity with his clients. He deplored the growth of the law factories, whose sole business came from large corporations and where lawyers were barely more than hired hands, with little respect or status. "I would rather have clients," he said, "than be somebody's lawyer." Just as those in need of legal services had the right to an attorney of their own choosing, so he believed lawyers could select those whom they wanted to represent, and he would not take on cases of dubious propriety. Because the nature of litigation often involved situations of competing rights, the Brandeis firm lost its share of suits. But Brandeis refused to serve a customer who had, in his opinion, acted improperly, and when he believed that one of his regular clients was in the wrong, he normally advised him to admit the error and settle out of court.

On a number of occasions Brandeis suggested to his clients that he might be of greater value as "counsel to the situation" rather than as an attorney for one faction or another. In such a role he attempted to strike a balance between the rights and obligations of each party and then work out a solution equitable to all. This judicial posture accurately reflected his efforts to create a new type of lawyer who could rise above partisan advocacy.

Once in a fight, however, Brandeis proved an extremely tough and durable opponent who had no qualms when going in for the kill. Like many men of quick and agile minds, he had little patience for fools and plodders, and he practically ignored the superficial socializing that occupied much time within the Boston bar. As a result he gained the reputation of a brilliant and rather ruthless lawyer, a lone wolf, something of an oddity in the upper strata of Brahmin Boston. Once after a long and bruising battle, he dismissed a lawyer dissatisfied with the outcome with a curt "Don't cry, baby." Such comments did little to endear him to his peers.

Other quirks also isolated him. Like many upper-class reformers, Brandeis had been a mugwump, bolting the Republican party in 1884 to support Grover Cleveland against James G. Blaine. He also joined the respectable Civil Service Reform Association and the Boston American Citizenship Committee. But his first real work as a reformer came in

1891, and the methods he chose, as well as the goals he sought, were a precursor to later endeavors.

The Massachusetts legislature, in spite of its reform tradition, was, like most other state assemblies in the Gilded Age, rife with corruption. Franchises, rights-of-way, permits, and other concessions needed by railroads and utilities were available to the highest bidder. To avert legislation that might harm them, corporate executives were quite willing to pay off legislators in order to have certain bills killed. The state's liquor dealers, for example, when faced by a growing temperance movement, fought back in the traditional manner by bribing enough legislators to kill the measure. The situation had become so bad, the bribery so open and flagrant, that a number of younger representatives, the "Young Democracy," called for a large-scale investigation of lobbying activities in the Bay State. One of these reformers, George Fred Williams, personally asked Louis to involve himself in their work.

Brandeis understood that very few controversies existed with one side totally in the right and the other completely wrong. He began to research the liquor issue, and he soon discovered that the reputed temperance measures before the legislature were so restrictive that if passed, they would put the liquor dealers out of business. Liquor abuse did exist, even the antitemperance people admitted that; few realized, or cared to discuss, that many of the liquor regulations already on the books were totally unworkable and unenforceable.

As it turned out, one of Brandeis's clients, William D. Ellis, served as the Boston agent of a large midwestern distillery and was an active figure in the Massachusetts Protective Liquor Dealers Association. Brandeis invited Ellis to his office and casually asked him to go over a list of legislators, marking off the names of those who could be bribed. With equal casualness Ellis did that, and as he handed the roster back to Brandeis, the attorney asked him: "Ellis, do you realize what you are doing?" Brandeis then launched into a sermon on the evils of bribery, until the agent was practically in tears. In response Ellis asked what could be done, and Brandeis outlined his plan. He would agree to become counsel to the Liquor Dealers Association on the conditions that Ellis be made chairman of the executive committee and that no expenditures be made without first consulting the new counsel. The Association agreed, and Brandeis went to work.

In February 1891 Brandeis presented a rather unconventional brief to the legislature's joint committee on liquor regulation, in which he asked for a revision of the state's liquor control laws. In personal testimony before the committee Brandeis pointed out the absurdities and inconsistencies of measures such as those which prohibited the sale of liquor except as part of a meal. Drinking liquor, he argued, was not wrong; drinking to excess was. Liquor sales should be regulated, but no regulation could be enforced if it was not reasonable. By passing unenforceable and unreasonable laws, the legislature had made criminals out of men who would much rather be obeying the law; moreover, it had forced liquor dealers to enter the political arena, in which they had no business, and it had fostered corruption. "You can make politicians of any class of people," he argued, "if you harass them, if you make it impossible for them to live unless they control, unless they have secured power to determine when and how and where they may live. You can remove liquor dealers from politics by a very simple device — make the liquor laws reasonable." Despite the opposition of the more extreme temperance advocates, the legislators recognized the innate common sense of the Brandeis proposal, and the ensuing legislation, reasonable and enforceable, did just what Louis had predicted: it removed the liquor dealers from the political scene.

This first venture into good government had about it nearly all the characteristics that would mark Louis Brandeis's progressive career. First, a careful review of the facts of the situation, followed by a plan equitable to all sides and, above all, reasonable and capable of being implemented. Brandeis was never a Don Quixote blindly tilting at windmills; when he entered the lists, it was with a determination to find a solution, not merely to decry the evil. "In all our legislation," he once told a congressional committee, "we have got to base what we do on facts and not on theory." Years later on the Supreme Court he would still be preaching this doctrine. "The logic of words," he lectured his brethren, "should yield to the logic of facts." The progressive era had more than its share of men and women who could cry out loudly and eloquently against real or imagined evils; it had too few who gathered facts, weighed the evidence, and then presented a workable plan to deal with the problem. Brandeis was one of this small group; he never attacked an evil without proposing a remedy.

Educating the legislature and the public was in many ways a far more important aspect of the Brandeisian reform. In the liquor issue the educational component was fairly limited — the informational brief, more concerned with explaining the issue rather than with the strictly legal arguments, personal testimony before the joint committee, and some minor public relations work. In later years Louis would develop the concept of a citizen lobby and base his campaign on a broad educational effort. No solution to any problem would suffice, he believed, unless the people understood the issue, unless they recognized why a particular remedy was the right way to resolve the difficulty. In the middle of his fight to secure savings bank life insurance, he wrote: "If we should get tomorrow the necessary legislation, without having achieved that process of education, we could not make a practical working success of the plan." A quintessential part of the progressive faith lay in the belief that the people would act to wipe out any evil if only they could be made aware of the problem. The success of a reform, therefore, depended on the educational program.

A final aspect of his reform style dealt with reimbursement. Few lawyers at that time engaged in public service work.

When the city of Philadelphia, for example, fought a corrupt gas company, it could not find a local attorney to handle the case and had to go to New York to secure legal representation. Brandeis was among the first, and the most conspicuous, to work *pro bono publico,* for the good of the public. Although at first he charged for his professional services and then donated the money to charity, he soon decided not to accept any payment for his public work. When Edward A. Filene tried to get a bill from Brandeis for his services in a traction fight, Brandeis evaded the issue for weeks and finally told Filene that he had resolved early in life to give at least one hour a day to public service, and later on he hoped to give fully half his time.

The idea of using his abilities for the public good was also part of his vision of the free life. "Some men buy diamonds and rare works of art," he explained, "others delight in automobiles and yachts. My luxury is to invest my surplus effort, beyond that required for the proper support of my family, to the pleasure of taking up a problem and solving or helping to solve it for the people without receiving any compensation. Your yachtsman or automobilist would lose much of his enjoyment if he were obliged to do for pay what he is doing for the love of the thing itself. So I should lose much of my satisfaction if I were paid in connection with public services of this kind. I have only one life, and it is short enough. Why waste it on things I don't want most? I don't want money or property most. I want to be free." For Brandeis the great happiness in life was "not to donate but to serve."

He did not see himself as an eccentric, however. Rather, he believed he was carrying out the traditional tasks and obligations of the lawyer, especially the mandate to provide justice for all. Brandeis by his example was asking lawyers to start making moral judgments, to stop turning their backs on complex situations. "What the lawyer needs," he declared, "is not more ability or physical courage but the moral courage in the face of financial loss and personal ill-will to stand for right and justice."

All these ideas could be found in his beginnings, in the early years in Louisville and Cambridge and Boston, in his establishment and success as a lawyer, in the initial forays into new forms of legal and public service. On an ever-widening stage he found new and greater opportunities to put them into effect.

II

The Reformer at Work

"I HAVE OPPOSED IT solely because I believe that the bill, if passed, would result in great injustice to the people of Massachusetts, and eventually great injustice to the capitalist classes whom you are now representing and with whom I, as well as you, are in close connection."

When Louis Brandeis wrote these words in May 1897, he quite explicitly aligned himself not with those who would radically alter society but rather with other successful people of his day who had prospered in a free enterprise system and who wished to defend and preserve capitalism. In this attitude Brandeis never wavered, and it is one of the ironies of his life that for more than four decades this essentially conservative man was denounced as a radical, as one who would tear down the free enterprise system. Yet progressivism at heart was conservative, striving to preserve established American society through moderate reform. Only by recognizing this conservatism inherent throughout the progressive era can we understand Brandeis and his reform work.

After the Civil War the United States plunged into a frenzied burst of industrialization. More than 60,000 miles of new rail tracks provided farmers and manufacturers alike with new markets half a continent away. Industries that had not even existed prior to 1860 sprang into being, as giant factories and mills gobbled up enormous amounts of raw material and spewed out wondrous new products of iron, steel, and copper. The frontier of opportunity shifted from the open lands of the West into the burgeoning cities. Chicago, which had a population of 28,000 in 1850, held a huge exposition in 1893 to mark its emergence as one of the nation's leading cities, home to 1.2 million people. Many sleepy outposts experienced similar growth; Cleveland, Detroit, St. Louis, and dozens of other cities mushroomed, attracting thousands of people seeking fame and fortune in their crowded streets.

The new urban populations contributed, in turn, to the growth of new industries. The local slaughterhouse gave way to the gigantic meat-packing plants of the Midwest, and Gustavus Swift made millions responding to the needs of city dwellers for fresh meat. James S. Bell built General Mills into a purveyor of grains to the millions. Peddlers still hawked their wares in towns and cities across the land, but more and more people began to order their clothing and tools and utensils from the Sears, Roebuck catalogue. The insatiable demands of new factories for iron, copper, and other ores spurred on the growth of Anaconda, Carnegie, and a host of metal firms, while John D. Rockefeller helped to light millions of homes by selling kerosene through Standard Oil outlets. To provide fuel for the factories, enormous mines were opened and expanded in West Virginia and Pennsylvania. Although farmers complained that they did not share in the new prosperity, the value of agricultural products rose from $2.6 billion in 1870 to $3.9 billion in 1900. All told, in the three decades following Appomattox, the gross national product jumped from $7.4 billion to $18.7 billion.

But a darker side marred the industrialization process. Factories poured out not only shiny new products but also waste matter into the air and waters of the nation, while the hunger for coal, wood, and minerals denuded millions of acres of land. To man the factories and mills and mines, millions of immigrants came to this land of promise, only to live in stinking city tenements or wretched hovels in mining towns that stretched across the country. Eight, ten, sometimes twelve people crowded into a single room, devoid not only of comforts but even of necessities. At the looms of mills weaving the nation's cloth, little children, some only seven years old, tended bobbins, while young boys in coal mines risked fingers and hands pulling breakers from the coal chutes. The men who dug out the earth's treasures worked twelve hours a day, seven days a week, year in and year out, rarely seeing the light of the sun. Their miserable existence oftentimes came to a brief, terrible end in cave-ins or explosions, or to a more lingering, painful death through black lung, the result of continuously breathing coal dust. In the cities tuberculosis slowly choked thousands of garment workers to death, while fire could claim dozens of lives in a conflagration such as the one that struck the Triangle Waist Company in 1910. Life was cheap, however, cheaper than installing safety devices. After the first flush of prosperity and of wonder at the material benefits of the new era, thoughtful men and women began questioning the costs, not only in human life and misery but also in regard to the effects the new industrialism was having on the social and political fabric of the nation.

The idyllic portrait drawn by Thomas Jefferson of a nation of yeoman farmers and independent craftsmen had never really existed, but parts of the myth had been true enough. So long as untold acres of rich western land could be had for a pittance, millions of men and women had been able to establish themselves as independent freeholders. The bright young lad who chose to stay in the city could, by hard work and ambition, hire himself out to a merchant or a draftsman, go on to be self-employed, and ultimately hire others to work for him. Not everyone prospered in America, but for a time the dream of rags to riches rested on the very real foundations of opportunity. In business, farming, or the professions, few obstacles stood in the way of those determined to succeed. In politics as well the great names of America's first century had been those who had risen to leadership primarily on the basis of talent.

As much as the degradation of the individual spirit in factories and mines, reformers feared the debasement of politics and society. A nation in which Mrs. Marshall Field, the wife of Chicago's department store magnate, spent more on one party than the shop girls in her husband's store could hope to make in a lifetime, had something intrinsically wrong with it. Legislatures whose members could be bought and sold, whose interests were narrow and selfish, could not sustain a democratic form of government. Worst of all, the new corporate enterprises choked off opportunity, making it impossible for young people to use their abilities and energies to carry them to the top.

Most progressive reformers had entered their careers toward the beginning of the age of industrialization and had been able to succeed before the gigantic companies came to dominate economics and politics. Whether or not they suffered a real or imagined slippage in status even while enjoying personal success is to some extent irrelevant. In their speeches and writing they bemoaned the change from the conditions they had known when young. "Half a century ago," Brandeis declared, "nearly every American boy could look forward to becoming independent as a farmer or mechanic, in business or professional life; and nearly every American girl might expect to become the wife of such a man. Today most American boys have reason to believe that throughout life they will work in some capacity as employees of others, either in private or public business; and a large percentage of women occupy like positions."

Progressives in general, and Brandeis in particular, sought to rein in the power of the new industrial giants, to limit their corrosive influence on the democratic process. They wanted to ameliorate the degrading effects upon the men, women, and children whose labors made business growth possible. In one way or another they sought to preserve what they saw as the essential decency and opportunity and equality of American democracy. No matter which particular reform effort one examines — be it mining and factory safety laws, hours and wage regulation, public health, conservation, or urban planning — the ultimate goal remained constant: to retard the negative aspects of industrialization while promoting a return to an earlier and better society. The roads to this goal varied considerably, and those called progressives often differed on the effectiveness or desirability of particular programs.

Louis Brandeis's road would touch upon many different reforms. At about the same time as his presentation for the liquor dealers, he undertook an investigation of pauper relief in Boston at the instigation of his friend, the philanthropist Alice N. Lincoln. His report anticipated the later progressive cry against the dehumanizing effects of modern society. "These people are not machines," he wrote, "these are human beings [with] emotions, feelings and interests. . . . Each one of them, and all of them, can be raised and raised only by holding up before them that which is higher and that which is better than they; . . . Men are not bad, men are not degraded, because they desire to be so; they are degraded largely through circumstance, and it is the duty of every man and the main duty of those who are dealing with these unfortunates to help them up and let them feel in one way or another that there is some hope for them in life."

Brandeis's first major reform effort came in 1897 when he tackled one of the more flagrant abuses of the new order. The rapid growth of cities had converted public transportation from a relatively minor business into a vital component of urban life. Moreover, technological improvements in the form of electric and steam trolleys now made it possible to tie together a sprawling metropolis, allowing businessmen and workers to move rapidly from one area to another. Suddenly the franchise for new trolley lines took on a very lucrative tinge, and the companies bidding for these rights did everything they could to secure franchises that would work entirely to their advantage and profit.

In 1897 the Boston Elevated Railway Company quietly secured a charter change from the state legislature, which would have given it nearly perpetual rights over certain desirable routes; in addition, the company was protected for twenty-five years against having to reduce its fare below five cents a ride. The bill was in the last stages of enactment when reformers caught wind of it, and in a public letter Brandeis called upon "all good citizens" of Boston to rally in order to protect their interests. The proposed changes, he argued, were "at odds with the established policy of the Common-wealth and would, if enacted, sacrifice the interests of the public to that of a single corporation." The protest came too late, however, to rally public opinion. Brandeis realized that to avert further losses, an alert citizenry had to remain ever watchful of situations open to abuse and fight at the first sign of danger.

Such signs appeared when the city built a subway under Tremont Street in the downtown business area and ordered the West End Railway to remove its surface tracks in the area so as to relieve congestion. Control of the subway and the large station into which nearly all of the Elevated's lines had to feed became the key to controlling Boston's transportation. As long as the city either kept control of the subway or leased it to the Elevated on reasonable terms, then the traction company's monopoly could be regulated; if the El secured a long-term lease entirely in its favor, then it could literally hold up the city for any price it chose. The issue was joined on the question of who would build and operate the Washington Street subway, the companion route that would complete the downtown system.

At first the Boston Elevated offered to build the subway, operate it for thirty years, and then give the city the option to buy it at cost, a proposal endorsed by the business-oriented Citizens' Association. But by now a new group had appeared in Boston, the Public Franchise League, a forerunner of the citizen lobbies of later years. Joining Brandeis in the League were some of the city's most civic-minded businessmen, in-cluding Edward A. Filene, Robert Treat Paine, Jr., and Dr. Morton Prince. Allied with the League in the fight was the Associated Board of Trade, and as unpaid counsel to the Board Brandeis appeared before the numerous legislative hearings. There was little doubt in anyone's mind, however, that his was the dominant personality in the entire traction battle.

The fight appeared almost to be lost when the Elevated offered to build the subway entirely at its own expense and then turn the completed system over to the city, which in turn would then allow the Elevated free and sole use of the line for fifty years. The legislature's Metropolitan Affairs Committee saw only one feature — it would not cost the city a dime in construction costs. The lawmakers favored the El's bill over the proposal offered by the Public Franchise League, which called for construction and ownership by the city, with a short-term restrictive lease to the traction company. Nearly all the Boston newspapers, with the exception of the *Post,* took a similar view; what did the terms of the lease matter so long as the city did not have to foot the bill?

On June 1, 1901, Brandeis wrote to Edward Filene, who had agreed to head a publicity bureau for the Public Franchise League. "In my opinion," he said, "our success will depend largely upon the thoroughness with which you may succeed." He then outlined a series of measures that, by current methods of influencing public opinion, seem crude indeed — a campaign of letters to editors, petitions from labor and civic organizations, messages to the legislature, all protesting the Elevated's proposal. Messages by the hundreds descended upon the legislators, and hardly a day passed without Boston newspapers carrying letters deploring the proposal. But the El also had its friends, and in late June it managed to push its bill through both houses of the state legislature. Only a veto by Governor Murray Crane could defeat the measure, and Brandeis made a personal appeal to the governor to do so. The efficacy of Brandeis's persuasive powers could be seen in Crane's veto message, which followed the Brandeisian argument in nearly every respect.

Defeating the Boston Elevated's plan, however, did not mean victory; the entire transit issue had to be resolved before the reformers could relax. Nor was the traction company about to surrender; in 1902 it launched a new campaign to secure an extended franchise, and once again it came close to achieving its goal. The Public Franchise League redoubled its efforts to generate public opinion, and Brandeis induced Boston Mayor Patrick A. Collins to support the League's bill. A crucial turn of events occurred when Brandeis was able to rebut a complicated financial argument submitted by the Elevated, which claimed that the company had lost money through its benevolent policy of free transfer. Even while the company's lawyer, Albert Pillsbury, delivered these hitherto unreported statistics, Brandeis, who once claimed that his special field was figures, was able to pierce the argument and show, using Pillsbury's own numbers, that the company had paid $600,000 in dividends, raising the rate from four to six percent, and that its stock had gone from 105 to 170 in less than four years — hardly the signs of a failing concern. Brandeis lectured the legislative committee in the finest Boston tradition: "We are here to see that the control rests with the community, that the Elevated Railway Company, or any company that serves us as transporters of passengers, is the servant and not the master of the public." A few days later the Public Franchise League issued a fifteen-page report prepared by Brandeis demolishing the El's claims of financial hardships.

This time the battle was won. The state legislature adopted the League's bill almost intact, authorizing the city to build the subway and then to lease it to the El for twenty-five years at an annual rate of 4.5 percent of cost. Both the traction company and the public, through a referendum, agreed to the plan. The city, however, did not stop growing, and at least three times in the next seven years the Boston Elevated attempted to secure sweetheart franchises to service new areas; each time Brandeis and the Public Franchise League intervened and made sure that the legislature did not grant any more than had been given in the Washington Street law.

In the traction fight Brandeis and the Public Franchise League took a primarily defensive posture, working to secure what they saw as a fair franchise in place of the exorbitant one demanded by the company. Although the League may have been right in principle, its plan in the long run did not make good economic sense. Supposedly at the end of twenty-five years the lease would be open to competitive bidding, competition being what Brandeis and many progressives saw as the heart of a proper economic system. But the conditions surrounding the delivery of public services are not, and should not be, the same as those in the private sector. Public transportation, water, gas, and other utilities are commonly conceded to be natural monopolies, with the most efficient and effective service available when one company controls the field. During the twenty-five years of the lease the El would have no competition. If it did badly, no one would want to take over the lease; if it did well, it could easily outbid any rival. Brandeis and his colleagues were right to seek a fair franchise, but their insistence on introducing a competitive model into Boston's urban transit ultimately proved damaging as well as unworkable. The League's next battle, however, displayed a more creative side of Brandeisian reform, one in which he proposed an innovative but economically viable solution to a problem in which both the public and private interests had legitimate rights.

The development of gas lighting introduced novel problems of political and economic abuse. Originally eight different companies supplied the Boston area with gas, and despite the surface appearance of competition, poor services resulted from incompetent planning, duplication of facilities, and a preoccupation by management with high profits on the one hand and political favors on the other. In 1903 the Boston Board of Gas and Electric Light Commissioners asked the state legislature to allow the eight companies to consolidate, with the stock of the new corporation to be limited to the fair value of the combined properties. Although some members of the Public Franchise League opposed the bill, the arguments for consolidation proved persuasive to the state's lawmakers, who approved the measure.

The main fight came the following year, when the new

Boston Consolidated Gas Company petitioned the city's utility commission for a property valuation of more than $24 million. Under the city law, gas rates would be set to yield a fair return upon the value of the property; the higher the initial valuation, therefore, the higher the rates the Consolidated could charge. At first Brandeis seemed unaware of the problem, but after prodding by Edward R. Warren, he assumed leadership of the fight and found himself struggling not only against the company but also against some of his own colleagues, who could not see all the problems involved. For this group, led primarily by Warren, only one issue mattered, that of property valuation; under no circumstances should the Consolidated be awarded a valuation higher than $15.1 million. This figure, they contended, represented the real value of the eight former companies; any larger sum would saddle the consumer with unwarranted high rates. They sought a target price of eighty cents per thousand cubic feet, twenty cents less than the prevailing dollar rate.

For Brandeis fair valuation was but one aspect of the situation. He saw gas service as a public utility, which had to provide the consuming public with the best service at the lowest possible price. At the same time Brandeis opposed public ownership of utilities and maintained that the stockholders in the Consolidated were entitled to a fair return on their investment. Although the valuation ought not to be grossly inflated, the businessman-lawyer recognized that a number of factors made the true replacement value of the property considerably higher than the original cost of $15 million. While leading the fight against overvaluation, Brandeis sought to find a means to protect the Consolidated's stockholders as well. First, however, the company and the regulatory board had to be stopped from fixing upon the $24-million figure.

Seeking a prior state experience upon which to base his argument, Brandeis turned to the Anti-Stock-Watering Act of 1894. Before the State Commission on Public Lighting he argued that the whole purpose of the law aimed at providing justice to the public and justice to the stockholder, protecting the first from the inequity of unfair rates based on gross overvaluation, and the latter from loss of security through debasement of property. He warned the company that the ultimate evils resulting from overvaluation and higher gas rates would more than offset short-term profits. "It is certain," he declared, "that among a free people every excess of capital must in time be repaid by the excessive demands of those who have not the capital. Every act of injustice on the part of the rich will be met by another act or many acts on the part of the people. If the capitalists are wise, they will aid us in the effort to prevent injustice."

Brandeis expected opposition from the gas interests, whose quest for unwarranted gas rates resulted from their short-sightedness. But he found an equally uncomprehending attitude among some of his colleagues on the Public Franchise League, who cared only for low rates and not at all for the real interests of the Consolidated stockholders. Eventually they parted company from Brandeis, and the breach widened after he came up with a novel solution to the problem, the sliding scale.

Originated in London, the sliding scale tied the rates of public utilities to their efficiency and in effect made the company and public partners. If a company increased its profitability, it could raise its dividends only if it also reduced its charges to the public. Under this system it would be practically impossible for a utility to overcharge or exploit the public, because increases in profits automatically triggered decreases in rates. The major concern of management centered on improving the efficiency of the company's operations.

Through the good offices of a mutual friend, Brandeis met with James L. Richards, the president of the Consolidated. A farmer's son who had made a fortune before he turned forty, Richards had been handpicked by the investment house of Kidder, Peabody to head the gas company and to look after the bankers' interests. Fortunately, Richards proved exceptionally open-minded, and he wanted to concentrate his energies upon building up the gas company, not on perpetually lobbying legislators to secure rate increases. He immediately grasped the idea of the sliding scale, and after several conferences he and Brandeis reached agreement on a bill that fixed the capitalization at $15.1 million, set the regular dividend at seven percent, and cut the cost of gas immediately from $1.00 to $.90 per thousand cubic feet. For every one percent rise in the dividend, the rates would have to be cut by five cents; because the Consolidated had been paying an eight percent dividend, this in effect meant that Boston would have eighty-five-cent gas within a year.

Both Richards and Brandeis now had to battle not only against enemies but against their erstwhile friends as well. Brandeis fought for the sliding scale bill in the legislature while carrying on a public exchange of letters, some quite bitter, with several of his disaffected allies in the Public Franchise League. Richards had his hands full trying to convince his banker friends that the sliding scale would protect their investments and that the Consolidated would earn a high rate of return even with reduced charges to the public. In the end the sliding scale passed the legislature and, after a public referendum, went into effect. As Brandeis had predicted, Richards's superb management brought Boston improved gas service at lower cost. Within eighteen months the company was able to raise its dividend to nine percent and provide Boston with eighty-cent gas, about the lowest rate for any major city in the United States.

The strange battle reflected Brandeis's concerns that all sides in a controversy should be treated fairly. He never considered the fight to have been only for fair valuation and low rates, although in the end he managed to secure a valuation and a rate below that of his one-idea colleagues in the Public Franchise League. Nor did he favor municipal ownership, although at one time he had been favorably impressed by the gas-and-water socialism of Henry George. Brandeis was a true capitalist, and he wanted investors to receive a fair and generous return on their capital, so long as they did not attempt to exploit the public. Finally, as in his first case for the liquor dealers, he wanted to remove business from politics. In an article for the *Review of Reviews,* "How Boston Solved the Gas Problem," Brandeis wrote: "The officers and employees of the gas company now devote themselves strictly to the business of making and distributing gas, instead of dissipating their abilities, as heretofore, in lobbying and political intrigue. . . . If the demand for municipal ownership in America can be stayed, it will be by such wise legislation."

Ultimately the gas victory cost Brandeis a great deal. His attempt to limit the excesses of capitalism led banking and business interests to consider him a radical, but his efforts to protect stockholders resulted in a number of former friends denouncing him as two-faced. Years later some of his bitterest critics in the confirmation fight would be these men alongside whom he had once fought. But if they could not grow, could not expand their vision, could not learn from experience, he could and he did.

The traction and gas fights taught Brandeis many things. First, the battle for reform never ended, neither after a victory nor after a defeat. New developments presented new opportunities, and if the reformers did not remain vigilant, the enemy could be counted upon to press every advantage. Second, he learned that virtue was not necessarily its own reward; working for the public good was as likely to bring opprobrium as praise. His had been a sensitive personality, and the abuse heaped on him greatly upset him at first. As he later told Norman Hapgood, he realized during the traction fight "that just as he was prepared to sacrifice the favor of that element in society which would make him the most money, so he must make himself indifferent to misrepresentation and never make any answers which would indicate any sensitiveness to abuse." It was a difficult decision to implement, yet a wise one; as Brandeis's career expanded to the national and even the international level, he would be subjected to a degree of calumny the young reformer never imagined possible.

Finally, Brandeis had begun to perceive the value, indeed, the power, of public opinion. Ten years earlier, in a letter to his fiancée, he had written: "All law is a dead letter without public opinion behind it, but law and public opinion interact and they are both capable of being made. . . . It is comparatively easy to make people believe anything, particularly the right." It had not proven to be that easy, but he now knew for certain that no reform could succeed without public support. How effective a weapon it could be for progressivism he proved in his campaign to establish savings bank life insurance.

Insurance companies were one of the great growth industries of the nineteenth century. From early and very limited beginnings as insurers of commercial risks, the industry had responded to a growing affluent middle class by providing insurance for life and property and had even developed a policy for workers. Industrial life insurance, though, was "the nearest thing to a racket ever run by respectable American businessmen." For a weekly premium of five cents or a multiple thereof, workers could purchase life insurance to protect their families. On the face of it, as the companies claimed, the procedure seemed fair enough, even public-spirited. Because workers allegedly could not afford the premiums for regular life policies, inexpensive term insurance, with easy-to-meet weekly payments collected by agents who even came to the workers' homes, filled a real social need.

A closer look, however, revealed facts that the companies tried desperately to hide. The cost of industrial policies, the so-called nickel premium, was actually much higher than that of regular life insurance, with a major part of the premium going to pay sales commissions. Moreover, the full amount of the policy did not come into effect for a year. If a workman bought a $500 policy, for example, and died within three months, his family collected nothing; if he died after three months, they received a fourth of the face value ($125); if he died after six months, they received half ($250). The industrial policies accumulated no cash value at surrender, and if a single payment was missed because of illness or unemployment, the company canceled the policy. From this system salesmen and the companies derived considerable gains; only the poor workers, with no other insurance options open to them, lost.

Brandeis became involved with the problem of industrial insurance in a rather indirect way. The billions of dollars held in reserve by the large insurance companies had proved an irresistible lure to many executives, especially in the Equitable Life Assurance Society of New York, where warring factions battled for control. The abuse in the management of the reserve pools, then being exposed by Charles Evans Hughes, led a group of Boston policyholders to form a protective committee to look after their interests. Brandeis agreed to serve as its counsel only after a stormy session in which they gave in to his demand that he be allowed to do so without compensation. As unpaid counsel, he explained, he would be able not only to look after policyholder interest but also to pursue possible avenues of investigation and reform that might not be of immediate concern to the committee.

In this reform Brandeis showed how very much he had absorbed the New England mentality. Aside from the abuse, why allow Massachusetts money to go to New York at all? Were there no local banks or investment houses or insurance companies who could manage Bay Staters' money in an efficient and profitable manner? Here is seen the same mistrust of Wall Street and its practices as could be found in the most conservative banking houses on Boston's State Street. We Boston people, both said in effect, can take care of ourselves and should be ashamed to let our money go outside the state.

Casting about for a model to prove his point, Brandeis hit upon the operation of the state's 188 small savings banks. In a speech to the Commercial Club of Boston in October 1905 (later widely distributed as a pamphlet entitled *Life Insurance — the Abuses and the Remedies*), Brandeis declared that on a pro rata basis it cost the insurance companies seventeen times as much to manage their investments as it did the state's savings banks, and the banks earned five percent more on their assets. All this had been accomplished not by great financial wizards but by the "obscure but conscientious citizens" who served as savings bank treasurers. To his secretary Alice Grady, Brandeis declared that the savings banks held the answer to the problem of industrial life insurance.

The establishment of savings bank life insurance, which Brandeis later characterized as his most socially useful and important reform contribution, was the prototypical Brandeisian reform. More than any other, it can serve as a case study of the progressive in action.

First came the identification of the problem, namely, that workers were denied access to affordable life insurance. The policies offered by the major commercial companies cost too much and did not offer even the normal benefits that middle-class consumers received in their programs.

Next came research to determine how great an evil existed and which of several potential solutions would best meet the needs of those affected. Much of the research Brandeis did himself while serving as counsel to the New England Policy-Holders' Protective Committee; he gleaned fact after fact from the annual reports of the companies and from government documents, such as the periodic audits and the statements of the Commissioner of Insurance. He also picked up valuable information from the Hughes Committee investigation. Brandeis's own research led him to believe that much of the companies' profits came not from their regular underwriting but from industrial sales. John R. Hegeman, president of Metropolitan Life, confirmed before the Hughes Committee that the cost of industrial insurance to the worker was twice that of regular life insurance, whereas Haley Fiske, Metropolitan's vice-president, openly admitted that the company came out about even on its ordinary business and made nearly all its profits on the industrial premiums. Forty cents of each dollar went into sales commissions and company costs rather than into the insurance reserve pool, and even the remaining sixty cents did not fully benefit the workers, because only one policy in twelve ever carried to maturity. The others lapsed, with the accumulated premiums going completely to the company.

Once Brandeis had documented the evils of the system, he needed facts to support his belief that the savings bank network could provide a low-cost life insurance program. He refused to be intimidated by the supposed complexity of insurance matters. "The business of life insurance is one of extraordinary simplicity," he declared. "To conduct it successfully requires neither genius nor initiative, and if pursued by the state does not even call for unusual business judgment. The sole requisites would be honesty, accuracy, persistence and honesty."

To prove this, he secured the services of Walter C. Wright, one of the country's leading actuaries. If Wright could provide the necessary statistics, Brandeis could then present a comprehensive plan to the special committee appointed by the legislature to investigate insurance. Back and forth went requests and responses, with Brandeis seeking the data to meet every potential objection that might be raised against the plan. Finally he had his figures, and on June 8, 1906, he circulated a manuscript to about a dozen friends and colleagues, seeking their comments and their support. With minor revisions Brandeis later published it as "Wage-Earner's Life Insurance" in the September 15 issue of *Collier's Weekly*, one of the country's leading reform journals.

In the article Brandeis spelled out not only the problem but the solution — the sale of life insurance through savings banks. There would be no sales agents and therefore no commissions; the overhead would be only a small increment to the banks' extant costs. As a result the cost of insurance could be cut drastically. Banks needed to assume only three elements in insurance: fixing the terms by which insurance would be provided, a task that could be done for the banks by a state actuary; examining the applicant, which could be done by a state doctor; verifying proof of death, which the banks already were doing in relation to accounts. Savings banks, distributed across the state and doing business with individual customers, were the ideal instruments to provide access to low-cost insurance; moreover, the resulting policies would have none of the defects of commercial industrial insurance. They would build up a redeemable cash value, and the entire face amount of the policy would be in effect from the day of issuance.

Predictably, savings bank life insurance was attacked by the insurance companies as either a wild-eyed, visionary, and impracticable scheme or as the dreaded first step on the road to socialism. It also had to face opposition from trustees and managers of the savings banks, who, rightly, were afraid to tamper with their institutions lest they endanger the assets of their depositors. To win legislative approval of the plan, Brandeis would have to generate popular support on a scale unparalleled in Massachusetts history and, at the same time, win over a majority of the trustees of several leading savings banks so that the plan could be implemented.

The campaign had actually begun with the publication of the *Collier's* article, which in one stroke gave the savings bank insurance proposal national exposure. Brandeis then under-took a heavy schedule of speech making, often talking several times a week, sometimes twice in an evening, in an attempt to win over civic, business, and labor groups all over the state. How much he had learned from his earlier efforts can be seen in the detailed letters he wrote during 1906 to the men handling local arrangements: if there were to be more than one speaker at a meeting, Brandeis should be scheduled to speak last; the key figures of the community, its leading citizens, should receive personal invitations to attend and, if possible, meet privately with Brandeis either before or after the public meeting; local newspapers should receive advance copies of his speech and be asked to send reporters to cover the meeting.

Throughout the year Brandeis kept up this pace, until by November 1906 he felt ready to organize the Massachusetts Savings Bank Insurance League with his friend Norman White, who had just been elected to the state assembly, as secretary. In the next few months the League enrolled more than 70,000 members, and its roster included hundreds of well-known figures in the Bay State. To emphasize the bipartisan nature of the organization, former Governor John L. Bates, a Republican, agreed to be one of the vice-presidents, and another former governor, Democrat William L. Douglas, served as president. The first step in the campaign to generate public support had proved immensely successful; one found backers of savings bank insurance in nearly every walk of life, in every city and town across the state, in civic and church groups, in labor unions and business clubs. The League was the first modern citizen lobby, and when the legislature met in the spring of 1907, Brandeis stood ready to use this new instrument to convince the lawmakers that the people of Massachusetts supported his plan.

The second step of the campaign proved much more difficult, winning the backing of savings bank officials; in fact, not a single bank had endorsed the idea after nearly a year of effort. Typical of the bank officials' sentiments are these comments of Joseph Shattuck, Jr., treasurer of the large Springfield Institution for Savings: "While I am open to conviction, I am opposed to having my bank enter a business for which it is not fitted. It appears to me that the average savings bank is a local institution only. The machinery of insurance would be costly even if there were a central association to keep us in touch with our policy holders in other parts of the state." Another bank officer declared that many of the depositors were barely literate enough to fill out a bank slip. How could they be expected to handle complicated insurance forms?

After several futile attempts to convince bank treasurers, Brandeis switched tactics to win over the institutions' trustees. The choice of Bates and Douglas as League officers did more than indicate the bipartisan nature of the reform. Douglas, the president of the People's Bank of Brockton, and Bates, a trustee of the Wildey Savings Bank, had easy access to other trustees. In early 1907 Douglas sent out a public letter calling for savings banks to endorse the insurance plan, and he got twenty-one of the twenty-four trustees of the Brockton bank to join the League. In February three more banks announced that if the legislature approved the proposal, they stood ready to put it into operation.

Now came the final step of the initial campaign, winning over the legislature. On January 3, 1907, Governor Curtis Guild, acting on Brandeis's request, called for the enactment of savings bank insurance, a plan he characterized as providing "cheaper industrial insurance that may rob death of half of its terror for the worthy poor." A few days later the Joint Recess Committee, which had hitherto been cool to the scheme, unanimously endorsed it. For the next five months the proponents of savings bank insurance kept up a steady stream of pressure on senators and representatives. The League's 70,000 members flooded legislative offices with cards, letters, and telegrams calling for enactment of the measure; individual legislators were lobbied, and careful selection was made as to which League member could most effectively persuade which lawmaker. In hearings before committees of both houses, Brandeis and his colleagues testified about the evils of commercial industrial insurance and the benefits that would accrue if the savings bank program were enacted. The trade journal *Insurance Post* had earlier written that "nobody need lose any sleep over the dream of the Boston theorist, for the dream has about one chance in a million of ever coming true." Now insurance company spokesmen were fighting desperately to stem the tide, only to find with each passing day that Brandeis's months of planning had generated an irresistible momentum in its favor. On

June 5, 1907, the enabling legislation passed the Massachusetts House of Representatives, 126 to 46, and on June 17 the Senate concurred 23 to 3. A little over a week later Governor Guild signed the bill into law.

Most of the advocates of savings bank insurance now considered the battle over; in fact, in many reforms in the progressive era, whether at the local, state, or national levels, few people ever saw past the legislative hurdle. One of Louis Brandeis's distinguishing characteristics as a reformer is that he realized the fight did not end until the program had actually been implemented, and even then it had to be watched carefully. Before Governor Guild had signed the bill, Brandeis had written to him suggesting possible names for the new system's board of trustees, to ensure that no enemies of the plan would have a chance to sabotage it from within. Moreover, the savings banks dragged their feet on establishing insurance departments; the plan was voluntary, and each bank waited for someone else to inaugurate operations, to see if Brandeis's scheme would really work. Not until June 1908 did the Whitman bank open an insurance department, to be followed in November by the Brockton bank. Once again Brandeis initiated a letter campaign, calling upon friendly editors to run articles and editorials on the merits of savings bank life insurance, directed toward influencing their local institutions to join the program. Though undoubtedly discouraged by the slow start, he understood the difficulties faced by bank officials, the reluctance of conservative men to commit themselves to new and untried ideas. All this took time, but over the ensuing years more and more Massachusetts banks joined the system.

One did not have to wait long, however, to see one result of the plan. In January 1907 the commercial companies cut the premium on industrial insurance by ten percent, and in July 1909 they reduced the charges by another ten percent, saving workers millions of dollars. In addition, some of the more obnoxious features of commercial insurance were eliminated. As Brandeis wrote to a friend: "Industrial companies have imitated our system in many of its particulars, as well as endeavoring to approach us on rates, and although the Metropolitan social department may be largely hypocrisy, it is to be borne in mind that imitation is the sincerest form of flattery, and hypocrisy the tribute which vice pays to virtue."

Brandeis kept a close eye on savings bank insurance. His secretary, Alice H. Grady, later became deputy commissioner of the system and consulted frequently with him. He remained vigilant, expecting that the commercial companies would not quit the field of battle, and he proved correct. Almost every year the industry introduced legislation limiting the amount of insurance that could be sold or proposed seemingly innocuous measures that in practice would have crippled the system. Each time Brandeis prodded the League and its supporters to fight back. The battle could never be considered completely won; the people had to remain ever vigilant to preserve their hard-won gains.

Brandeis never saw savings bank insurance as a radical measure; rather he viewed it as essentially conservative, "progressive" in the truest sense of the term. He opposed federal supervision, believing that local governments should be the main focus of regulatory activity; national laws would only strengthen the power of the central government, a trend at which Brandeis already looked askance. "The great captains of industry and of finance," he declared, "who profess the greatest horror of the extension of government functions, are the chief makers of socialism." The abuses in industrial insurance posed a much greater danger to the free enterprise system than did government involvement by a local regulatory agency.

Nor did Brandeis wish to replace private with government insurance. The system would be voluntary, would operate through the quasi-private savings bank network, but would be subject to strict supervision by a state board of trustees. Competition should, as indeed it did, force the commercial insurers to offer a better package and function more efficiently. In later decades this concept came to be known as a yardstick, embodied particularly in the Tennessee Valley Authority. The idea was never to socialize the industry or force it out of business but only to make it operate better.

Working class men and women would, of course, profit from lower premiums, but beyond that their independence would be strengthened. In a letter to Judge Warren Reed, Brandeis explained that "what we want is to have the workingman free, not to have him the beneficiary of a benevolent employer, and freedom demands a development in the employees of that self-control which results in thrift and in adequate provision for the future." Here the conservative in Brandeis recognized that a permanent proletariat, totally servile to and dependent upon corporate employers, constituted a great threat to capitalism. Only by providing opportunity and freedom, by instilling essentially middle-class values and goals for the workers, could the system continue to grow and prosper.

In the gas consolidation and the savings bank insurance Louis Brandeis proved a creative as well as an effective reformer; he not only fought an abuse but provided a workable solution to the problem. In his fight against the New Haven merger he was the economist as moralist.

The New York, New Haven and Hartford Railroad had long been a major component of New England's economy, and its stock was perhaps the classic widows-and-orphans investment, a blue chip that had paid an annual dividend of eight percent or more for decades. Nearly all the major State Street banking houses held large blocks of New Haven in their portfolios, and its list of directors included many pedigreed Boston families. This identification between the Brahmin elite and the New Haven explained why Brandeis became the target of their venom during his campaign against New Haven policies, for it appeared he was attempting to drag down a mainstay of their society. What remains inexplicable is their refusal to acknowledge the facts he exposed, the poor physical and financial condition of the road, which threatened their own investment; moreover, Brandeis based his arguments on the most valued of New England's traditions, fiscal probity.

A Massachusetts law of 1874 had forbidden railroads to hold "directly or indirectly" stock in other corporations. The New Haven, which by 1905 had come under the domination of the Morgan interests, not only had begun buying up stock in the urban street railways but had also acquired nearly a third of the shares of the Boston & Maine Railroad, the other major line in New England. The New Haven attempted to achieve its goal using holding companies, or as New Haven President Charles Sanger Mellen put it: "Interests identified with my company have acquired a large stock interest in the Boston & Maine Railroad." Other stockholders in the B & M, however, opposed this takeover, and they retained Brandeis as their counsel. Once again sensing the large issues involved, Brandeis agreed to serve only if there were no fee; he wanted complete freedom of action.

Nothing in his past experience had quite prepared him to take on the New Haven. Then at the height of its political and financial power, the road employed a bevy of publicists and had an impressive list of the right people ready to defend the merger. The reputation of the line as a well-managed and prosperous company gave much credence to its argument that an integrated and efficient transportation network for the region, not monopoly, was its goal. Perhaps the greatest weapon in the New Haven's arsenal was its president, Charles Mellen, whose advocacy of the benefits that would flow from the merger of the two lines mesmerized many people.

The battle began in earnest in the 1907 legislative session, when Brandeis proposed a bill requiring the New Haven to dispose of its Boston & Maine stock by April 1, 1908, and making it a criminal offense for the road to purchase additional shares. For the first time Brandeis began to expound his opposition to large corporations, which he believed threatened the political as well as the economic well-being of the community. Where the merger advocates saw the benefits of a unified transportation system, Brandeis feared the creation of a power beyond the reach of legislative safeguards, a power that, through its control of New England's major railroads, would literally hold the region by its throat. Although the New Haven easily killed the Brandeis bill, it could not secure legislative sanction for the merger; instead, the line accepted a measure that allowed it to hold the B & M stock for another year, until some final disposition might be worked out. For Brandeis the coming year would be one of fact gathering, for as he explained to his brother in October 1907: "I think before we get through, the estimable gentlemen who scrambled for the chance of exchanging their B & M stock for New Haven will find that they have been served a gold brick. At the present stage of investigation it looks as if Mellen . . . will run up against a stone wall as soon as his borrowing capacity ends. There are some indications that it has ended (with his stock at 139) and that he is resorting to all kinds of devices to get money. I have not been able to figure out yet from data available what he has done with all the money he raised and should not be at all surprised to find that some has already gone into dividends."

When the New Haven's annual report came out, Brandeis found the document riddled with inconsistencies and marked by glaring gaps of information. Piecing the story together with the help of material from the Interstate Commerce Commission and the Massachusetts Railroad Commission, he published a pamphlet in 1907 that charged the New Haven with covering up massive financial losses. Had the road followed standard accounting practices, he claimed, it would have been unable to pay its regular dividend. As for the B & M, which the merger advocates had claimed would benefit from the union, it was financially in much better shape than the New Haven. The real purpose of the New Haven, in fact, was to get hold of the B & M's assets to cover its own losses. Unless the New Haven mended its ways, Brandeis forecast, it would have to reduce its dividend.

The pamphlet exploded like a bombshell in State Street. The New Haven and its allies quickly counterattacked, charging that Brandeis, with no training in accounting, had absolutely no facts to back up his ridiculous accusations. The entire community, or so it seemed, now turned against this despoiler who cast aspersions on the great New Haven. "I have made a larger camp of enemies than in all my previous fights together," Louis wrote to Alfred. He must also have wondered somewhat at the parochialism of his Boston neighbors, who instead of seeking to determine whether his charges were true or not, closed ranks to defend their own.

The very shrillness of the New Haven response assured Brandeis that his facts were correct, and so he set out again on the difficult road of stirring up public opinion. A few weeks after the pamphlet appeared so did another Brandeis creation, the Massachusetts Anti-Merger League, modeled on the successful savings bank insurance lobby. But the public seemed much more confused about the merits or dangers of railroad merger than it had been about the evils of industrial insurance. Although the Anti-Merger League generated a great deal of material and kept the salient facts before the community, it never commanded wide support. Instead of the campaign building upon a wide base in the community, it nearly always remained the cause of a relatively small group of businessmen and antimonopolistic reformers.

The reason for the lack of public support lay in the complexity of the merger proposal and the fact that despite Brandeis's efforts many people in the community did not see the merger as a simple matter of good or evil. Opponents labeled the union of the two roads monopolistic, but a number of other lines serving the region, such as the Boston & Albany or the Vermont Central, remained free from New Haven control. Moreover, many people recognized the need for unified service for the region, a prospect that required close connections if not an actual merger between the Boston & Maine and the New Haven. The latter's reputation for sound financial management, as well as its massive public relations campaign, obscured the facts that it had not made sufficient profits to justify its high dividends and that it had made drastic cuts in maintenance and repairs to save money. The road needed the resources of the B & M, a fact that Mellen could not admit. In the end the merger opponents won because the New Haven tried to violate not only the laws of Massachusetts but the rules of arithmetic as well.

The New Haven suffered its first series of setbacks in May 1908 when the Massachusetts Supreme Court ordered it to divest its trolley lines, a decision that left little doubt that a similar decree could be expected regarding the B & M stock. A few days later the newspapers discovered that a previously favorable report by the Massachusetts State Commission on Commerce had actually been drafted in large part by Charles F. Choate, Jr., the New Haven's attorney. Moreover, even fancy juggling of figures could not hide the fact that in order to pay its April 1 dividend, the line had had to dig deeply into reserves. Seemingly the final blow came when antimerger forces in the House of Representatives secured passage of a bill requiring the New Haven to divest itself of B & M stock within two years. This sudden turnaround in the New Haven's fortunes surprised not only Mellen but Brandeis as well, who in a most satisfied manner told Mark Sullivan in June that "our victory is complete."

For once Brandeis relaxed too soon. One month after passage of the divestiture law the New Haven sold its stock to John Ballard of Meriden, Connecticut, a move that seemed perfectly lawful. Over the next year, however, the New Haven lobby worked quietly but effectively, gaining support for a bill chartering a company whose sole purpose would be to hold stocks and bonds of the Boston & Maine Railroad. With the backing of Governor Eban S. Draper, the bill cleared both houses of the legislature. Ballard now sold back his stock to the new holding company, which, of course, was completely owned by the New Haven. The merger Mellen had sought evidently had been achieved.

Brandeis maintained public silence while he switched his battleground from Boston to Washington. There his contacts with insurgent congressmen, led by his new friend Robert M.

LaFollette of Wisconsin, allowed him to launch new attacks from a broader platform. On April 12, 1910, for example, LaFollette flayed the New Haven in a speech replete with data only Brandeis could have supplied. Beyond that, he induced the Interstate Commerce Commission to investigate the New Haven, and the subsequent ICC hearings verified each and every one of Brandeis's earlier accusations. Using its independent investigators and its subpoena powers, the ICC discovered that the Ballard deal had been fraudulent from the start; without putting up a penny of his own, Ballard had made $2.7 million for holding B & M shares until the New Haven could push through its new bill. Auditors took the road's financial reports apart and soon confirmed Brandeis's analysis — the New Haven had been operating at a deficit for several years, first digging into reserves and then borrowing money in order to pay its dividends. Supposedly independent personalities who had defended the New Haven and the merger, including one professor at Harvard, were shown to have held regular and large retainers from the line. In order to save money, the line had neglected essential repairs on track and equipment, leading to an alarming rise in accidents. As one item after another came into the open, New Haven stock dropped precipitately. In its final report on July 9, 1913, the commission concluded: "Had the stockholders of the New Haven, instead of vilifying the Road's critics, given some attention to the charges made, their property would today be of greater value."

The seemingly impregnable empire of Morgan and Mellen collapsed, with the once proud New Haven permanently ruined. Within a week after the ICC hearings the line reduced its dividend to six percent; six months later it omitted its quarterly dividend for the first time in more than forty years, and except for brief interludes during the boom times of the 1920s, it would never pay profits again. By then Mellen had gone, resigning from the presidency of the Boston & Maine on July 8, 1913, and from that of the New Haven nine days later. Two years earlier Brandeis had predicted the course of events and, in a letter to Norman Hapgood, suggested a moral for the story:

When the New Haven reduces its dividend and Mellen resigns, the "Decline of the New Haven and the Fall of Mellen" will make a dramatic story of human interest with a moral — or two — including the evils of monopoly. Events cannot long be deferred and possibly you may want to prepare for their coming. Anticipating the future a little, I suggest the following as an epitaph or obituary notice:

Mellen was a masterful man, resourceful, courageous, broad of view. He fired the imagination of New England, but being oblique of vision merely distorted its judgment and silenced its conscience. For a while he triumphed with impunity over laws human and divine, but as he was obsessed with the delusion that two and two make five he fell at last a victim of the relentless rules of humble arithmetic.

Remember, O Stranger!

Arithmetic is the first of sciences and the mother of safety.

In the New Haven battle Brandeis began to articulate a well-developed philosophy regarding the evils of bigness. Long before the drama closed with the ICC hearings, Brandeis had begun to broadcast these views on a wider stage, and in 1912 he found a most receptive audience in the Democratic candidate for president, Woodrow Wilson. But by then Louis Brandeis was no longer just a local reformer, a municipal do-gooder. Even as he carried on the fight against the New Haven, he was establishing a national reputation as the people's lawyer.

III

The People's Attorney

THE PASSION THAT YOUNG Louis Brandeis had held for the law did not diminish as he grew older; rather it increased as he came to a greater understanding and appreciation of the role of law in a free society. Even as he built up his successful practice and began devoting time to reform work, Brandeis remained a man for whom the law constituted much more than legal machinery, mere means toward ends. The law and its study represented one of the highest forms of intellectual activity, while its practice allowed people to resolve their differences in an orderly and civilized manner.

But the law could be effective as a guarantor of social peace only if it remained relevant to social needs. As the country changed, as its economic and political institutions matured, the law also had to make adjustments. Moreover, the practitioners of the law, attorneys and judges, had to realize their grave responsibility in keeping the law abreast of the times. The fundamental principles should not be tampered with; rather, basic tenets had to be retained while modifying the manner in which they were applied. Yet at the turn of the century as he looked around him, Louis Brandeis saw an increasingly reactionary bench and bar which refused to acknowledge the existence of change, and whose concerns focused almost entirely on the preservation of private property and its attendant privileges. In challenging these attitudes Brandeis surely appeared as a radical, a defiler within the temple; yet once again a closer examination reveals the true conservative at work.

By the 1890s the legal profession had come to serve Mammon as God. A creed of laissez-faire and freedom of contract, wrapped in the sacred mantle of the Constitution, had elevated property rights to an unprecedented level. William Ramsey triumphantly proclaimed the new dogma to his fellow attorneys: "The right to contract or to be contracted with . . . is sacred, and lies at the very foundation of the social state." All efforts to protect people from the abuses of property ran afoul in courts that consistently ruled that the Fourteenth Amendment precluded any and all infringements on the supreme rights of property. State and federal laws that attempted to protect labor, promote social welfare, or foster human rights were held unconstitutional. In Wisconsin Judge James G. Jenkins prohibited workers not only from striking but from quitting their jobs, because such action would infringe upon the property rights of their employers.

This law came down from on high. Justice Stephen J. Field worked assiduously in the United States Supreme Court, so that on the one hundredth anniversary of that institution he could unequivocally declare that the main business of the Court was enforcement of property rights. Professor Thomas McIntyre Cooley, in the most influential legal text of the times, amplified the doctrine of implied limitations on all government powers where they infringed upon property. Within the bar associations leading lawyers such as William Guthrie told their colleagues: "We lawyers are delegated not merely to defend constitutional guaranties before the courts for individual clients, but to teach the people in season and out to value and respect individual liberty and the rights of property."

Brandeis did not stand alone in his opposition to those who would bar any social improvements at the expense of sacred property rights. Several other legal progressives, nearly all of whom had been influenced by Oliver Wendell Holmes's 1880 Lowell Lectures on "The Common Law," also worked to break down the wall between law and social progress. In this group, however, Brandeis soon achieved recognition not only as a spokesman but as a practitioner of the new jurisprudence.

Brandeis's first essays on legal philosophy, a series of articles in the *Harvard Law Review* in the 1880s on privacy and water rights, grew out of very practical concerns, the needs of a working attorney for information on a new subject. But the pieces won the attention of scholars and lawyers alike for their innovative and commonsensical approach to complex matters. As he grew increasingly aware of social problems in the late 1890s, however, Brandeis also became more concerned with the rigidity of legal thinking. The law had not kept apace of the times; lawyers and judges had refused to acknowledge great changes in the world.

"Political as well as economic and social sciences," he declared,

noted these revolutionary changes. But legal science — the unwritten or judge-made laws as distinguished from legislation — was largely deaf and blind to them. Courts continued to ignore newly arisen social needs. They applied complacently eighteenth-century conceptions of the liberty of the individual and of the sacredness of private property. Early nineteenth-century scientific half-truths like "The survival of the fittest," which, translated into practice, meant "The devil take the hindmost," were erected by judicial sanction into a moral law. Where statutes giving expression to the new social spirit were clearly constitutional, judges, imbued with the spirit of individualism, often construed them away. Where any doubts as to the constitutionality of such statutes could find lodgment, courts all too frequently declared the acts void. . . . The law has everywhere a tendency to lag behind the facts of life.

Was it any wonder, therefore, that the courts had been under attack, that the common people perceived lawyers and judges as tools of the rich? Approvingly Brandeis quoted Lowell's words:

New times demand new issues and new men,
    The world advances, and in time outgrows the laws
That in our fathers' time were best.

New times had indeed come, and the law had lagged behind. The real vitality of the law, the aspect that more than anything else made people willing to live by its rules, derived from its relevance to what Holmes had called the "felt necessities of the time." Although there would always be some gap between social change and legal adjustment, this gap had grown so great in the late nineteenth century as to threaten both the law and society. Brandeis and other legal progressives asked only that a "living law," not a petrified jurisprudence, correct this disjuncture.

For the law to live, it had to treat with reality and not with myth. Both as a lawyer and later as a judge, Brandeis frequently quoted the old legal maxim that "out of the facts grows the law." Only by following this precept, he suggested, could the courts preserve their integrity and have people respect their decisions. As early as 1891, in the liquor lobby brief, he had lectured the Massachusetts legislature that "no law can be effective which does not take into consideration the conditions of the community for which it is designed." To a congressional committee twenty years later he repeated this message: "In all our legislation we have got to base what we do on facts and not on theories." And once on the bench he admonished his colleagues that "the logic of words should yield to the logic of realities."

But for the courts to "yield to the logic of realities," the judges had to know what these realities were. "A judge is presumed to know the elements of law," he once wrote, "but there is no presumption that he knows the facts." The responsibility for making sure that the judge had all the relevant information rested with the lawyer presenting the case, and the lawyer, therefore, had to be trained not only in the law but in economics, sociology, history, and other nonlegal fields. The true men of the law, the great jurists, required inquisitive minds which ranged far beyond narrow legal questions.

Brandeis expected that lawyers, by educating judges, would help secure decisions more in tune with a society in flux. But lawyers had a larger role to play in preserving the rule of law, and he castigated the profession for abandoning its duties in this area. "Instead of holding a position of independence between the wealthy and the people," he charged, "able lawyers have, to a large extent, allowed themselves to become adjuncts of great corporations and have neglected their obligations to use their powers for the protection of the people. We hear much of the 'corporation lawyer' and far too little of the 'people's lawyer.' The great opportunity of the American Bar is and will be to stand again as it did in the past, ready to protect also the interests of the people."

A number of themes, therefore, came together in the one case more than any other associated with Louis Brandeis's name, *Muller* v. *Oregon* (1908). The tasks of bringing the law and reality into consonance, of educating judges to the facts of life, of representing the public — all united to produce a new means of legal argumentation. Although reformers, lawyers, and scholars have lauded Brandeis's innovative presentation for decades, the real brilliance of the Brandeis brief lay in its attempt to harmonize the law, which is in essence conservative, with the need for social change.

Brandeis's sister-in-law, Josephine Goldmark, and her associate in the Consumers' League, Florence Kelley, had approached him to defend an Oregon law establishing a ten-hour workday for women. He agreed on two conditions: first, that he officially represent the state of Oregon in the proceedings before the United States Supreme Court and not just act as an amicus curiae (friend of the court) through the Consumers' League; second, that the League provide massive amounts of data regarding the effects of long working hours upon women. Most lawyers believed that the Oregon statute would be struck down by the high court, which had invalidated a New York ten-hour law in 1905. In the *Lochner* case, however, the Court had conceded that the police power of a state could be invoked if circumstances warranted. Brandeis realized, therefore, that the *Lochner* decision did not have to be reversed; rather the legitimacy of the Oregon law, its justification by facts, would have to be established.

Muller marked a crucial point in Brandeis's career. He

would challenge the highest bastion of legal reaction, and if he lost, the gap between law and life that he so deplored would widen further, leaving the legal reactionaries in even greater control. On a more personal level, his legal philosophy, his demand that lawyers represent the public as well as corporate clients, his very reputation, all hung in the balance. *Muller*, as few other cases, would have major and immediate repercussions on both legal thought and social reform.

The ten-hour law struck at the heart of the conservative creed, the idea of liberty of contract. If a person wanted to work twelve, fourteen, or even eighteen hours a day and could find someone willing to hire him, then both parties were free to contract such an arrangement. But the reasoning that underlay this concept, that both parties to the contract stood on equal footing, had been undermined by the Industrial Revolution. The village blacksmith and his hired hand may have been roughly equal; no parity existed between the United States Steel Corporation and its unskilled laborers, a fact that the law had failed to acknowledge. Oregon, in its statute, put forth the argument that if, in fact, all parties to a contract were not equal, then the state, acting through its police powers, could limit the right to contract in order to protect the weaker parties.

Such reasoning the legal and economic conservatives could not concede. Joseph H. Choate, a pillar of the New York bar, declared that he could not understand why a strong, husky Irish laundrywoman should not work more than ten hours a day if she so wanted. He feared that if Oregon's infringement upon liberty of contract were sustained, other restrictions on hours for men, on working conditions, and even on wage levels would come next. A philosophy of laissez-faire demanded that no matter how unequal the game, the state should not interfere. Equality before the law was thus carried to its logical, yet patently unfair, extreme.

In his brief in the *Muller* case Brandeis devoted a scant two pages to legal citations, and more than a hundred to employment statistics. The *Lochner* decision had held out the possibility of court approval if justification could be shown; this Brandeis did by citing one study after another on the effects of long working hours on the health and morals of working women. He did much more than just argue the case for Oregon; he tried to get all sides to understand why the state had passed the law, why it was necessary, how it justifiably utilized the police power. He advised the Court, and in doing so he lectured the learned justices on matters about which they knew little yet which were essential to their understanding of the case. From *Muller* onward lawyers could no longer evade their responsibilities of instructing and advising the courts on the relevant facts.

Years later the very conservative Mr. Justice George Sutherland commented that Louis Brandeis was the greatest technical lawyer he had ever encountered. No mere technician, however, could have written the brief Brandeis presented in *Muller* v. *Oregon*. Admittedly he had the help of Josephine Goldmark and Florence Kelley in gathering the data, but it took a master craftsman to transform those thousands of shards of evidence into a complete, logical statement of the accumulated wisdom on the subject. He educated his fellow lawyers as well as the judges not in legal syllogisms but in a very simple fact: women were different from men. Here was Brandeis the educator in action, instructing bench and bar in what the law should be and, more important, why it should be that way.

The decision in *Muller,* upholding the Oregon statute, allowed social reformers to hope for further advances. But *Muller* was only the beginning of the fight, not the end, for the legitimacy of regulating hours would be challenged repeatedly in the courts. Brandeis took part in defense of an Illinois law in that state's courts, and he successfully defended an Ohio statute on women's hours in *Hawley* v. *Walker* (1914). He also argued on behalf of minimum wage legislation in *Stettler* v. *O'Hara* (1916), but the victory in that case proved illusory. Seven years later, when his disciple Felix Frankfurter presented a Brandeis brief, the Supreme Court voided a federal wage statute in *Adkins* v. *Children's Hospital*. In that case Justice Sutherland relied heavily on the *Lochner* precedent, ignored *Muller,* and dismissed Frankfurter's massive presentation of data as interesting but irrelevant. In 1936 the Court severely limited the state's regulatory powers in the *Tipaldo* case. The next year, however, by a five-to-four vote, the Court reversed itself and validated minimum wage legislation in *West Coast Hotel* v. *Parrish*. Brandeis, then in his twenty-first year on the bench, thus lived to see the arguments regarding law and social need that he had set forth three decades earlier finally confirmed.

Brandeis's reputation as an attorney concerned about people rather than corporations grew considerably in the years following the *Muller* case. By 1910 he had all but given up private practice of law to devote himself to reform work, although he still drew over $100,000 annually from his firm for cases he brought in. His willingness to take on big businesses and to defend social legislation, as well as his refusal to accept payment for this work, brought him national exposure. More and more his morning mail included letters from reformers across the nation seeking advice on how to put Brandeisian techniques into effect in their own cities and states. In the late 1890s he had found himself flooded with private business; now his large firm handled legal matters while he strove to keep up with demands for his aid in progressive causes. Two matters in particular are worth close examination because they reveal Brandeis at work in his chosen field. One displays the creative lawyer, the other the tenacious investigator.

On March 4, 1909, William Howard Taft took over the presidency from Theodore Roosevelt, and in appointing a relatively conservative cabinet, he upset some of Roosevelt's more progressive followers. Perhaps the nomination that worried them most was that of Richard A. Ballinger as secretary of the interior, the post that controlled the extensive mineral and forest lands Roosevelt had put aside in national trust. The conservationist group's suspicions rose in August when Ballinger reopened for sale valuable coal deposits in Alaska, the Cunningham claims that Roosevelt had withdrawn.

Louis R. Glavis, head of the General Land Office's field agents, suspected collusion between some Interior Department officials and the Guggenheim mining interests, and he reported his fears to Ballinger. When the secretary dismissed the report, Glavis turned to Chief Forester Gifford Pinchot, who suggested that Glavis send on the facts he had gathered to Taft. The president and his Interior secretary then went over the materials, together with Attorney General George W. Wickersham and Oscar M. Lawler, an assistant attorney general assigned to Interior. As a result of these conferences, Taft completely exonerated Ballinger from any charges of wrongdoing, and he told him to dismiss Glavis. Realizing that some conservationist noses would be put out of joint by this action, Taft privately appealed to Pinchot not to get involved; the matter was no more than an attack by an insubordinate official without supporting evidence.

Pinchot, however, did not agree, and on November 13 *Collier's* published Glavis's original report, which triggered a national demand that Congress investigate the whitewash. Progressive forces learned, however, that the Taft administration would attempt to manipulate the hearings by stacking the committee with Republican stalwarts; moreover, once Ballinger had been cleared, he planned to sue *Collier's* for $1 million in libel damages. In response Robert J. Collier retained Henry L. Stimson and George Wharton Pepper, both eminent corporation lawyers, and at editor Norman Hapgood's suggestion he also brought in Brandeis as a private counsel, at a fee of $25,000 plus expenses. In the end Stimson withdrew, Pepper played a subsidiary role as lawyer to Gifford Pinchot (who ignored nearly all his advice), while Brandeis, technically the attorney for Glavis, directed the progressive side.

On January 12, 1910, Brandeis set himself up at the New York Harvard Club and in a by now familiar pattern began to familiarize himself not only with details of the Cunningham claims but with the workings of the Interior Department as a whole, its regulations and the laws delineating its powers and responsibilities. According to some employees of the agency, by the time Brandeis appeared at the congressional hearings, he knew as much, if not more, about the Department as did most of the men who had spent years working there. On January 26 hearings began in the old Senate Office Building under the chairmanship of Knute Nelson of Minnesota, an outspoken supporter of the administration.

Taft was far from the anticonservationist villain depicted by his contemporary critics; in his one term in office, for example, he reserved more timber and mineral lands than Roosevelt had put aside in nearly eight years. Moreover, the real battle, totally obscured by partisanship and the efforts to whitewash Ballinger, revolved around competing philosophies of public land management: the Pinchot group believed in preserving public lands inviolate, to be used only by nature lovers and occasional sportsmen; Ballinger and his aides favored planned usage, with timber and mineral resources developed in a manner and at a rate to maintain the quality of the reserves while the nation benefited from their products. In the long run Ballinger may have been correct; later philosophies of land management have, for the most part, espoused controlled exploitation of resources.

For Brandeis, however, the philosophical question, at least temporarily, took a lower priority than ferreting out the truth in Louis Glavis's charges. The Pinchot-Ballinger controversy became the political arena in which progressives fought the forces of reaction. This was how it appeared to the participants, and what might and ought to have been a dignified debate over policy and philosophy turned into a quasi-investigation-cum-circus.

The Republican stalwarts attempted from the start to block access to information as much as possible; Brandeis and his allies had to fight constantly for permission to secure documents and cross-examine witnesses. Although the hearings had originally been called to see whether Glavis's charges had been true or not, the party faithful felt — correctly — that the insurgents wanted to put the Taft administration on the defensive; instead of Glavis having to prove that what he said was true, Ballinger would have to prove that he had acted in innocence.

The hearings started slowly, but in early March the investigator in Brandeis began to sense something wrong in Taft's clearance of Ballinger. According to the administration story the president and the attorney general had received the Alaskan land record and supporting documents on September 6, 1909. Taft issued his statement a week later, based upon a summary and report by Wickersham dated September 11. Brandeis believed that it was physically impossible for the report to have been written in so short a time, because the record and documents ran more than a million words and the report itself consisted of seventy-four pages of small print. Brandeis doubted that the attorney general could have done this work so fast even if he had devoted all his time to it, and Wickersham had certainly been involved in other activities during that time. He suspected that in fact the document had been prepared well after Taft had cleared Ballinger on September 13. Internal evidence also cast doubts on the report's dating; one section referred to a charge Glavis had not made until much later.

The issue, at least in Brandeis's mind, now boiled down to whether the Taft administration had been truthful in its dealings with the American people, or if it had lied to cover up wrongdoing by one of its officials. The question, he told the committee, is "not merely whether Mr. Ballinger was properly exonerated, or whether Mr. Glavis was properly condemned, but whether, after the events that occurred on September 13, steps were taken with the idea of making that appear proper which was not proper when done. The question is of far more importance than the question of the correctness or the error in the original proceedings."

Brandeis now called for more and more documents from

the administration, papers that supposedly had been prepared prior to Wickersham's report, and the increased resis-
tance he met only reinforced his suspicions. On each and
every vote the Republicans denied his requests by a seven-to-
five count; only if he could secure proof on his own, proof so
conclusive that the administration would have to yield to his
requests for documents, could he verify his suspicions. While
searching for that evidence, he continued to subject administration witnesses to withering cross-examination, forcing
them to admit that politics had played a major role in many
Interior Department appointments and that a number of key
positions, including that of the secretary, had gone to men
who had prior business connections with the very interests
they were now supposed to regulate. Ballinger himself had
earlier done extensive legal work for the Guggenheims in
relation to the Cunningham claims. Every so often Brandeis
would manage to insinuate a question regarding the timing of
various reports, and every day he would renew his request for
papers, only to meet the same Republican denial. Finally,
however, he found his evidence.

A young stenographer in the Interior Department,
Frederick M. Kerby, had known the true story for some time.
But Kerby had a family to support, and disclosure of his
information would cost him his job. When he managed to
secure another position, he prepared a lengthy memorandum for Brandeis's use. Ballinger, not Taft, had written the
letter the president had signed exonerating the Interior
secretary, and the supporting materials allegedly provided by
Attorney General Wickersham for Taft had not been ready
until well after September 13.

Kerby's statement ran in the newspapers on May 14; that
same day Wickersham suddenly found a letter from Oscar
Lawler confirming that a draft had been prepared for the
president. Taft, informed of Kerby's charge but unaware of
what his attorney general had done, issued a statement
together with Ballinger totally denying Kerby's version of
events. The duplicity that Brandeis suspected had occurred

the previous fall had been repeated; by attempting to cover one lie with another, the administration now appeared to have been corrupt on all the issues. The suspicions of the conservationists no longer seemed silly or unfounded; rather the president and his closest advisers had been shown to be untrustworthy.

To the conservatives the villain of the drama was not Kerby but Brandeis, whom Lawler accused of stooping to irresponsible and underhanded tricks, even of having gumshoes follow members of the administration. Senator Elihu Root, who had fought Brandeis throughout the hearings, put the question to the Boston attorney directly: Did he have a detective shadow Secretary Ballinger? Brandeis assured the senator that this had not been the case. His extraordinary knowledge of the daily activities of the president and his cabinet members had been gleaned from the most ordinary sources — regular reports of the president, Ballinger, and other high government officials appeared in various New York, Washington, and Boston newspapers. By paying attention to details and collating the newspaper accounts, Brandeis and his aides had been able to reconstruct an almost hourly account of where these men had been and what they had been doing. This summary, minute in detail, gave Brandeis the information he needed to bolster his charges that Taft and Wickersham could not possibly have digested all the relevant documents and put together their reports in that one week in which they claimed to have done so.

Despite the admission of duplicity, the committee, by its usual seven-to-five majority, voted to clear Ballinger, but the administration's victory soon turned sour. The press, carefully supplied by Brandeis with incriminating data, kept up pressure on Taft and Ballinger. The people's attorney believed "that there is a great desire [by the people] to know, and to have stated in a clear and accurate form, what was developed in the investigation." He sent out hundreds of copies of the brief prepared in Glavis's defense, and in private letters as well as public statements he reiterated his demand for probity in government, for individual responsibility and accountability. In his closing argument to the committee he summed up his case this way:

We want men to think. We want every man in the [government] service, of the three or four hundred thousand who are there, to recognize that he is part of the governing body, and that on him rests responsibility within the limits of his employment just as much as upon the man on top. They cannot escape such responsibility. . . . They cannot be worthy of the respect and admiration of the people unless they add to the virtue of obedience some other virtues — the virtues of manliness, of truth, of courage, of willingness to risk positions, of the willingness to risk criticisms, of the willingness to risk the misunderstandings that so often come when people do the heroic thing.

In this argument Brandeis expounded two of the basic tenets of the progressive faith, that people are not innately wicked, only ignorant, and that for the people to act correctly, to do the right thing, they must be informed about the facts of the matter. To secure this public information, however, those in positions of responsibility had to be willing to do the courageous thing, even at the risk of personal loss, so that the greater good of the public might be served. The ideal of professional, efficient government, so much a part of this period's reform, rested on the assumption that good people, doing the right thing, would ultimately educate the public to follow their lead.

Ultimately public clamor forced Ballinger to resign in March of 1911, but it did not stop the business interests seeking access to public lands from continuing their campaign. Before Ballinger left office, the government approved transfer of nearly 13,000 acres surrounding Alaska's Controller Bay to the Guggenheim interests. The bay area would be crucial in any development of the Cunningham fields, for it provided the major outlet for shipping the coal to market. Several reporters scented another scandal, for Richard S. Ryan, the Guggenheim agent, had allegedly worked the deal with the aid of the president's brother, Charles P. Taft. A damaging Dick-to-Dick letter from Ryan to Ballinger, allegedly uncovered by an investigating reporter, could not be found in either the Interior Department or the White House files, and the president, his credibility badly damaged by the earlier disclosures, heatedly denied that any such document existed or that he had ever talked to his brother about the Alaskan development. With the incident following so closely upon the Pinchot-Ballinger affairs, however, insurgents in Congress needed little prompting to launch a new investigation. This time Brandeis would be in a much better position to secure information, for he had accepted an invitation from Representative James M. Graham, chairman of the committee, to serve as its unpaid counsel.

Again the familiar scenario began, but this time Brandeis had the assistance of several well-trained lawyers and reporters, including Amos Pinchot, Gilson Gardner, Myrtle Abbott, and John Lathrop. After familiarizing himself with the facts about the Chugach National Forest (of which Controller Bay was part), he assigned his aides to tracking down the activities of Ryan, Charles Taft, and others for the preceding year. Moreover, they were to compile a full record of the Morgan-Guggenheim syndicate's operations in Alaska. With his troops deployed, Brandeis looked at the calendar and, realizing that August had arrived, left for a vacation in the New Hampshire mountains.

Unlike the earlier investigation, where he had concentrated almost entirely on ferreting out official wrongdoing, Brandeis now devoted more time and thought to the broader considerations of public policy. He sketched out a comprehensive proposal for Alaskan development, one that would safeguard the territory's natural resources while giving the frontier settlers opportunities for social and economic growth. In a lengthy memorandum to Robert M. LaFollette, Brandeis spelled out a plan that combined public ownership of utilities, government protection of lands, and parameters for the role of private enterprise. Although neither man realized it, both

Brandeis and Ballinger favored similar goals — namely, controlled development of Alaska — but differed considerably on the extent of private and public sector involvement and responsibility.

Little came of these ideas at the time. Walter L. Fisher, an old friend of Brandeis's who succeeded Ballinger as secretary of the Interior, went on a personal fact-finding tour of Alaska and upon discovering irregularities forced the Guggenheims to withdraw their entries on Controller Bay. Brandeis's own examination of the allegations regarding the administration's activities and the role of Charles Taft showed up a number of inaccuracies in the published newspaper allegations. Although the government may have acted unwisely, he informed Representative Graham, no evidence existed that it had acted unlawfully. And so the investigations of Taft's conservation policy came to an end, with no clear resolution of the great problem of Alaskan development.

By then, however, Brandeis found himself involved in a new, and for him a unique, problem. The New York garment industry was a chaotic melange of small manufacturers, home workshops, individual piece goods contractors, and competing labor unions. Many employers had banded together in a Cloak, Suit and Skirt Manufacturers' Protective Association, which spoke for the companies but had no real power over any of its members. The makeup of both employer and employee groups derived almost entirely from the great wave of eastern European Jews that had come to the United States after 1880, and the workers in particular were heavily imbued with a socialist ethos. Cutthroat competition, atrocious working conditions, and the irregularities of a seasonal industry had spawned bitter employer-employee relations, which in turn sparked dozens of strikes and walkouts. By the summer of 1910 conditions had so deteriorated that the various worker groups decided to call a general strike, with a closed shop at the top of their list of demands.

The garment manufacturers, for the most part, seemed ready to fight indefinitely, but the industry's customers, especially the large department store owners with limited inventories on hand, feared the effects of a major strike. A. Lincoln Filene, a Brandeis client, asked the attorney to intervene in the strike on behalf of the store, but Brandeis refused to act unless the workers dropped their demand for a closed shop, a demand he had condemned years earlier as undermining the basic concepts of industrial democracy. After a lengthy series of negotiations with owners and unions, Filene managed to secure agreement from both sides to invite Brandeis in as a mediator. He agreed to talk to the parties, and at the first round of conferences he got the General Strike Committee of the unions to withdraw its call for a closed shop on the understanding that the essential rights of labor unionism would be protected. The spokesman for the shop owners immediately distorted this to mean that the unions had conceded the major point, and he referred to Brandeis as "attorney for the union in this strike." The workers in turn denounced this apparent double cross, and they threatened to stay out for weeks or even months until all their demands were met.

Fortunately, cooler heads prevailed. Samuel Gompers, president of the American Federation of Labor and an old acquaintance of Brandeis, urged the more radical strike leaders to seek compromise and assured them that Brandeis was indeed a friend of organized labor, a man they could trust to keep his word. Meyer London, the union's lawyer, and Julius Henry Cohen, acting for the employers, sent a joint telegram to Brandeis on July 27 asking him to chair a meeting of the warring parties. For days Brandeis used his utmost tact and persuasive power to prevent a deadlock. He started with the least controversial issues, seeking agreement where possible and holding contested items for future discussion. As often as possible he let the combatants talk themselves out, interrupting periodically to seize upon even the most minor points of agreement. Just when it appeared that the deadlock would be broken, however, John B. Lennon, one of the more militant labor leaders, demanded that the garment makers agree to the closed shop. Despite Brandeis's feverish efforts to steer the negotiations back to less controversial topics, the union men refused to cooperate, and the meeting broke up with both sides as far apart as before.

For Brandeis the closed shop presented a number of problems. By making it impossible to hire anyone but union members, it unfairly restricted the right of employers to hire the best people. Beyond that, he believed that the unions confused means and ends. The end they really wanted was an organization, recognized by worker and employer alike, which would protect the workers and negotiate on their behalf for better pay and working standards. Workers would voluntarily join a union once they saw the benefits it could gain for them. To force laborers to join a union in order to secure employment, however, violated his ideas of democracy.

As a compromise Brandeis offered a "preferential union shop," an idea he had unsuccessfully attempted to introduce in a 1907 strike in Boston. The employers, when hiring new workers, would give preference to union members over nonunion workers if their qualifications were equal, but they would be free to hire nonunion applicants who showed superior abilities. A mediation board would police the agreement to be sure that the employers were not discriminating against union people. At first the preferential union shop met a cool reception from both factions. The manufacturers did not like any arrangement that involved union membership in employment considerations, and the unions failed to see that intermediate positions did exist between the extremes of open and closed shops. Despairing of agreement, Brandeis wrote to his brother that "the outcome is doubtful, with probabilities that there will be no settlement because of the union demand for an all-union [closed] shop."

Probably the only things that saved negotiations were the faith both sides had in Brandeis's goodwill and his refusal to participate in the bitter accusations that now flew back and forth between the warring groups. Gradually they came to recognize that Brandeis spoke only for himself, that he was indeed acting as a neutral counsel to the situation. Henry Moskowitz, a New York social worker and reformer, clearly depicted this when he wrote that Brandeis "has made a profound impression on both sides. He will kill his standing with the workers if the judicial silence is broken. I have no doubt he feels the same way. His capital importance to the labor movement in America is more essential than a statement at the present juncture." While Brandeis returned to his vacation, Filene, Moskowitz, and other peacemakers worked upon both parties, and in the end Brandeis's original proposal for a preferential shop, in only slightly modified form, won acceptance.

The protocol settling the strike, which was signed on September 2, 1910, called for the creation of the preferential union shop and for joint employer-union machinery to police the agreement. A seven-member Joint Board of Sanitary Control would establish standard working conditions throughout the industry. Shop committees consisting of worker and employer representatives would settle disputes in individual factories, with a Board of Grievance serving as an appeals court. Should the Board fail to settle any issues, no strike or lockout could be called until the matter had been heard by a court of last resort, the three-member Board of Arbitration. Since the Board would be the key element in ensuring industrial peace, its makeup would be crucial to the success of the protocol. Everyone involved — unionized workers, manufacturers, and retailers — agreed that only one man stood qualified to serve as the Board's chairman, and Brandeis acceded to their invitation.

In its first few months of operation, however, the protocol almost ran aground. Both sides interpreted its terms to suit their own attitudes and wanted to take every minor issue right to the Board of Arbitration. Brandeis, in turn, refused to convene the Board, insisting that if the protocol were to work, all but the most intransigent issues had to be settled by either the local shop committees or the Board of Grievance. Industrial democracy demanded a give-and-take between employers and employees, not a constant appeal to outside arbitration. So long as both sides failed to understand that, the built-in governance apparatus could not work, and grievances accumulated until Brandeis had no choice but to call a meeting of the Board of Arbitration. At this session, on March 4, 1911, he refused to allow either side to indulge in rhetoric, insisting that they present nothing but the basic facts in each case. It soon became clear to everyone that nearly all the cases should have been handled in either the shops or by the Grievance Board. With the concurrence of Hamilton Holt, representing the manufacturers, and Morris Hillquit, the union member of the Arbitration Board, Brandeis directed that the lower levels of the grievance machinery be strengthened.

Once that was done, the protocol began functioning in the way Brandeis had hoped it might. Most disputes never went beyond the shop committees; the Board of Sanitary Control established uniform standards, which slowly brought some order out of the once chaotic industry. The preferential shop strengthened organized labor, with ninety percent of the workers joining unions, but it still allowed individuals the choice of whether or not to affiliate. In the next few years the idea of the protocol spread to other parts of the garment industry in New York and to other cities. Henry Moskowitz, now the Arbitration Board's clerk, joyfully wrote nine months after the signing of the protocol: "Substantial progress has been made by both sides . . . they are getting together more and more [and] developing efficient modes of negotiation; good feeling seems to be strengthening on both sides."

Smooth operation of the protocol, however, required nearly continuous policing as well as high degrees of goodwill, organization, and sophistication on all sides. Troublemakers could therefore easily magnify real or imagined difficulties. By early 1913 the grievance machinery had nearly collapsed under the assault of the more radical union organizers, who charged the conservative leadership of the Ladies Garment

Workers Union with collusion with the manufacturers. Brandeis, by now occupied with national matters for the Wilson administration, had little time to devote to his role as chairman, and when he did act, it proved too late. The spirit of cooperation, the rock upon which the protocol depended, gave way as both unions and employers took increasingly inflexible and antagonistic positions. The protocol dragged on until the summer of 1916, when it crumbled in another general strike.

In the end unions and manufacturers blamed the protocol, and Brandeis in particular, for failing to stand firm on crucial issues. Neither side recognized that the protocol was a mechanism for providing industrial peace, provided both employers and unions really wanted peace. So long as each group felt it could not compromise, then the protocol had no chance of ultimate success. Part of the blame undoubtedly rested upon Brandeis, and he recognized this. After the demise of the protocol he wrote to Julian Mack, a colleague in the peace machinery: "I dare say either of us, if we could have been constantly on the job in New York, might have made things move more smoothly." But to have industrial peace rely on the constant intervention of a supreme arbitrator ran directly counter to the mutuality and trust the protocol had been designed to foster — and without which it could never succeed.

IV

The Architect of the
New Freedom

BRANDEIS HAD FOUND by 1912 a larger cause and a
leader he respected. He first met Woodrow Wilson at Sea
Girt, New Jersey, on August 28 of that year. The people's
attorney had originally supported the presidential aspirations
of his close friend Robert M. LaFollette, but after the senator's collapse, Brandeis paid closer attention to the onetime
history professor's campaign. A number of Brandeis's progressive colleagues had urged him to join them in backing
Theodore Roosevelt, but Brandeis could not go along with
them. In Wilson he discerned the rough outline of an economic and moral philosophy closely akin to his own. Shortly
after Wilson won the Democratic nomination, Brandeis wrote
to congratulate him, and soon afterward he received an
invitation to lunch. At that meeting, which lasted more than
three hours, the two men discussed the major issues confronting progressive reformers, and more important, each took
the measure of the other. The Sea Girt conference marked a
turning point in Wilson's campaign and, although Brandeis
did not realize it, dramatically affected his own future as well.

Wilson had at one time been an economic conservative who
believed that progress meant rightness; what survived, therefore, was good. As late as 1908 he condemned any sort of
government regulation of the economy as socialistic in principle, sure to be followed by government ownership. He

praised the newly emergent trusts for "adding so enormously to the economy and efficiency of the nation's productive work," and he described them as "the most convenient and efficient instrumentalities of modern business." But beginning in 1907 a new strain crept into his economic commentaries, a strain based upon Wilson's stern Protestantism. Wilson spoke for a rising middle class that viewed the economic system not only as a means of production and distribution but also as a moral system, in which honesty, efficiency, frugality, hard work, and perseverance were tested and rewarded by material success. But as more and more of American business organized into gigantic firms, less and less room remained for the individual to compete. Wilson spoke for a middle class being squeezed out by big business, for young men beginning their careers with no room to rise.

By the time he ran for governor of New Jersey in 1910, Wilson had accepted many of the basic premises regarding monopoly then being expounded by the muckrakers. But he had no plan for dealing with big business, and he rather naively suggested that corporate evil could be combated by dragging it into the light of public opinion. In one interview he suggested that much of the furor over business could be eliminated if corporate executive meetings were subject to public scrutiny; individuals would do no wrong if their sins were out in the open for all to see. Wilson would play on this theme time and again, emphasizing the individual's obligation to control his actions in the light of an absolute standard of morality. His secular concept of sin was selfishness, and he often referred in his speeches to the dichotomy between action and morality. In dealing with the cause of monopoly, Wilson tended to attack individuals rather than economic conditions. When he won the Democratic presidential nomination, he had no other solution to offer than to establish a rule of justice and to enforce the criminal provisions of the Sherman Act.

Despite this vagueness in Wilson's thinking, Brandeis recognized that essentially they both sought a society free from the domination of either big government or big business, with a competitive, small-unit economy offering opportunities to those with skill, ambition, and courage. The people's attorney could offer the presidential candidate an articulate program on how to deal with monopolies, which would avoid the pitfall of big government inherent in Theodore Roosevelt's New Nationalism.

Brandeis had long been thinking seriously about the problems of big business and the effect of concentrated economic power on a free society. Monopoly, he believed, resulted from unregulated competition, a marketplace in which no effective checks prevented the strong from destroying the weak. While Brandeis, like Wilson, believed that the market provided a testing ground, he rejected the Darwinian notion that the strong, surviving by any means, were the best. Reason and morality imposed limits on the competitive struggle. Brandeis also held that political democracy depended upon economic democracy. "We must remember," he told the U.S. Chamber of Commerce, "that we are working here in America upon the problem of democracy, and we cannot successfully grapple with the problem of democracy if we confine our efforts to political democracy. . . . The [American] ideal which we have can be obtained only if side by side with political democracy comes industrial democracy."

Brandeis always maintained that old established American ideals remained valid even in a highly complex society. Where Wilson feared larger economic power for economic reasons, Brandeis opposed it on social and political grounds. If economic power could become strong enough to destroy liberty, then a countervailing power had to be established. "Those who wield a large amount of power," he declared, "always shall feel the check of power. The very principle on which the nation exists is that no person shall rise above power." His studies of railroads and industries persuaded Brandeis that there were limits on size beyond which business grew less rather than more efficient. Therefore, he proposed breaking up the large trusts and establishing rules in the marketplace to ensure a fair, but spirited, competition.

Brandeis presented most of these ideas to Wilson at Sea Girt and discovered he had an apt pupil. When reporters crowded around the two men afterward, Brandeis simply stated that they had discussed industrial problems, and that he would support Wilson because he found him "in complete sympathy with my fundamental convictions." Wilson noted that "both of us have as an object the prevention of monopoly." Then in words new to him, Wilson went on to declare that "monopoly is created by unregulated competition, by competition that overwhelms all other competitions, and the only way to enjoy industrial freedom is to destroy that condition." In his search to restore this freedom he had called in Mr. Brandeis who, more than anyone else he knew, had studied "corporate business from the efficiency to the political sides."

Wilson soon began using Brandeisian ideas and phrases in his campaign speeches. He attacked Roosevelt's program of government regulation of monopoly and asked: "What has created these monopolies? Unregulated competition." The answer, Wilson declared, lay not in government control but in remedial legislation to "so restrict the wrong use of competition that the right use of competition will destroy monopoly." A few days later he attacked monopoly as destructive not only of economic but of political freedom, and he argued that the only alternative to regulating monopoly was to regulate competition. But on the meaning of unrestricted competition and on a solution the Democratic candidate remained embarrassingly vague.

In late September Wilson journeyed to Boston to speak at the Tremont Temple. Before the speech he conferred with Brandeis, and a new note crept into his attack. "There is a point of bigness," he declared, "where you pass the point of efficiency and get to the point of clumsiness and unwieldiness." Wilson, however, now appeared inconsistent, since he had long maintained that he did not oppose bigness per se, only bigness attained illegally and immorally, as in a monopoly. To Brandeis, on the other hand, the "real curse was bigness rather than monopoly"; he later recalled that Wilson attacked monopoly rather than just bigness for political considerations — "Americans hated monopolies and loved bigness." In an attempt to clear up this inconsistency and also to delineate his views on Roosevelt, Wilson asked Brandeis to "set forth as explicitly as possible the actual measures by which competition can be effectively regulated." Brandeis drew up a lengthy statement that set forth the points that he and Wilson agreed upon and also summarized the opposing views of Roosevelt's Progressive party. The Bull Moosers saw monopoly as desirable and beneficial, while the Democrats upheld competition. Roosevelt believed that the excesses of big business could be prevented by government regulation, while Wilson should argue "that no methods of regulation ever have been or can be devised to remove the menace inherent in private monopoly and overweening commercial power."

Wilson concurred completely with the philosophy but considered some of the proposals enumerated by Brandeis too specific for a campaign. William Gibbs McAdoo, Wilson's campaign manager, then suggested that Brandeis work up the notes into articles to air the proposals without incurring any political liability for Wilson. In the next few weeks *Collier's* ran several articles under Brandeis's signature, while other pieces appeared under the guise of editorials by Hapgood. Wilson studied the articles carefully, and at this point the two men's views really converged. The memorandum called for a society grounded on a small-unit, highly competitive economy. In the past such competition had been ruthless, leading to a survival of the fittest. But the most fit in terms of survival may not have been the most fit in terms of morality. When America underwent the pains of economic maturation, many unethical practices prevailed, and monopolies resulted from the advantages such practices bestowed. Both Brandeis and Wilson believed that economic freedom undergirded political independence. "No nation can remain free," said Wilson, "in which a small group determines the industrial development; and by determining the industrial development, determines the political policy."

Illicit competition — that is, competition involving unfair practices — had led to monopoly and therefore, a priori, was bad. Wilson and Brandeis did recognize that at times superior efficiency and quality could also lead to monopoly. In some cases, as in public utilities, monopoly was natural and desirable; in such instances, however, it had to be strictly regulated in the public interest. But to Brandeis the limit of efficiency stood as a natural barrier preventing good business that was big from becoming monopoly that was bad.

Wilson and Brandeis totally opposed Roosevelt's New Nationalism; they objected to the Rough Rider's proposal to legitimize monopolies and then have a big government regulate their activities. The New Nationalism favored economic cooperation; the New Freedom believed in competition on moral as well as economic grounds. Roosevelt argued for the greater efficiency of the large unit; Wilson spoke for the democratic value of the small unit. Brandeis recognized that small units might be wasteful at times, but democracy itself was a wasteful system; political liberties, however, more than compensated for these wastes. Wilson and Brandeis desired a greater individual liberty under a simplistic government, while Roosevelt called for a strong social organism, superior to the individual, in a system designed primarily for efficiency. Carried to extremes, one program could lead to anarchy, the other to fascism.

The Brandeisian approach appealed to a southerner who believed that a government governs best when it governs least. Big business, basically inefficient, was socially less desirable than small, individual enterprise. Government, with a minimum of interference in the economy and the society, would establish rules of competition and thus prevent monopoly. Wilson could have his cake and eat it, too — small enterprise and limited government. No one, however, not even Brandeis, knew how to define or measure this superior efficiency, or where to draw a line beyond which large corporations would lose, rather than gain, in efficiency.

But size alone was not the problem; the progressives feared the concentration of power that bigness created and centered in just a handful of firms and individuals. By 1899 monopolistic groups accounted for nearly a third of the value added by industry to the gross national product. In the next fifteen years the figures grew even more alarming. The concepts of concentration, combination, and control dominated American industry. The debate, therefore, involved real questions: Should the country follow the Rooseveltian doctrine of accepting the facts of large-scale enterprise and subject it to governmental regulations; or should it follow Wilson's call to reverse the trend, reestablish a basically competitive society, and regulate that competition? By choosing Wilson, the voters expressed not only a choice of economic policy but one of psychological and moral alternatives as well. As Jackson nearly a century before had rooted up and thus destroyed the Bank of the United States, so they now hoped Wilson could root up and destroy the trusts.

Following the election Wilson sought a place for Brandeis in his cabinet and instinctively thought of the attorney general's office, a position from which the Bostonian could mount a sustained attack on monopoly. As the president-elect told his confidant, Colonel Edward M. House: "Ive got to have men in the cabinet who have passed the acid test of honesty. Men who are brave. Men who are efficient. Men who have imagination." As rumors of the appointment spread, progressives and social reformers praised the choice. Senator LaFollette sent a message to Wilson that Brandeis, more than anyone else, could "pull together the progressives — whether LaFollette, Democratic or Bull Mooser — and harmonize progressive legislation." Secretary of State designate William Jennings Bryan, the elder statesman of the Democratic party, assured Wilson that no better man could be found. "He has a standing among reformers and I am quite sure all progressives would be pleased." No man mentioned for appointment to the cabinet, not even Bryan, had such wide support from all reform elements.

But Brandeis had made many enemies, and they rose in turn to denounce the idea of a radical as the government's chief legal officer. Boston financier Henry L. Higginson, who had clashed with Brandeis in the New Haven affair, wrote to his friends that "we must stop the chance of his being taken." A. Lawrence Lowell, the president of Harvard, and other pillars of New England society warned Wilson that Brandeis had no standing among the best people and that he had a reputation as an unethical lawyer. So vehement was the protest that Wilson wavered, fearful of placing so controversial a person in so sensitive a position. He gathered some of the allegations against Brandeis and asked journalist Norman Hapgood to find out the truth.

Brandeis, well aware of the rumors, had mixed feelings about entering the government, because any official position would limit his freedom to act. As he told his brother: "I concluded to literally let nature take its course and to do nothing either to get called or to stop the talk, although some of my friends were quite active." As to the opposition from financial interests, he found it "quite amusing how much they fear me, attributing to me power and influence which I in no respect possess."

Undoubtedly some of the men who opposed Brandeis disliked him because he was a Jew, but the main opposition came from those who feared his views on big business, men who had been the targets of his antitrust and other reform activities. Nearly all the letters that poured in to Wilson, either praising or denouncing the anticipated appointment, dwelt on Brandeis's record as a reformer.

Wilson finally decided for political purposes not to name Brandeis as attorney general. Wilson had been elected by only forty-three percent of the voters, a plurality that hardly provided a solid base from which to launch his legislative program. A Brandeis nomination would alienate much of the commercial community, whose support would be crucial for the success of proposed banking and business measures. Moreover, the Democrats had been out of the White House for twenty years, and Wilson was beset by demands for patronage from the party chieftains. Brandeis had never been a party man, and in his battles for good government he had made enemies of Massachusetts Democrats as well as Republicans. Even a suggestion that Brandeis might be named to the less influential Commerce Department raised a storm of protest. The outcry from business leaders, conservative Democrats, and party leaders led Wilson reluctantly to shelve plans for Brandeis in the cabinet; three years later Wilson, in a much stronger political position, would not back down from his plans to place Brandeis on the high court.

The turnabout brought sorrow to the progressives and joy to business leaders. It "breaks all our hearts," wrote LaFollette, and several of Brandeis's friends wrote to him that their hopes for the Wilson administration had been dimmed by this knuckling under to business interests. In banking and business offices, on the other hand, a general sense of gratification prevailed. Both sides failed to realize that Brandeis had so influenced Wilson and had so earned his confidence that the president would rely heavily on his advice whether he was in the cabinet or not.

The New Freedom's attack on monopoly took three forms: tariff revision, currency reform, and a strengthening of the antitrust law. Wilson chose to attack the tariff problem first because the Democratic party stood united on that issue and it seemed the best place to start. There is no evidence that Brandeis advised the president on this matter, but on currency reform and trust law Brandeis exerted a powerful and decisive influence. Wilson knew very little about banking and finance. He called the concentration of fiscal power in Wall Street "the most pernicious of all trusts," and as such the solution had to be political as well as economic. By his inauguration Wilson had evolved certain basic premises, chief of which was that a money trust of monopoly proportions existed and to restore competition it had to be destroyed. Brandeis's series of articles, "Other People's Money," derived from the findings of the Pujo committee, confirmed Wilson's belief in the existence of a money trust; he read the pieces carefully, making notes in the margins.

In his message to Congress Wilson made destruction of this monopoly in order to restore competition the major purpose of the legislation. Reform should make banks the servants, not the masters, of business. It would not be enough merely to destroy the monopoly, nor even to guarantee it would not be re-created; the interests of the people had to be protected through governmental supervision. Shortly afterward Wilson gave his tentative approval to a plan devised by Carter Glass and H. Parker Willis, which called for a decentralized, privately controlled reserve system of not more than twenty independent reserve banks. The president made several additions, the most important an "altruistic Federal Reserve Board in Washington to supervise the proposed system," a capstone to it. In general the Glass-Willis plan was cautious and conservative, aimed at winning the support of a broad spectrum of respectable business and banking leaders, with control of the system and of currency remaining in private hands. Frequently consulting with Wilson, Glass and Willis worked the bill up in the spring of 1913; the president submitted it for serious consideration by inner administration personnel in early May.

Secretary of State William Jennings Bryan immediately condemned the proposal on two grounds and, together with attorney Samuel Untermyer, began drawing up a more radical program. First, under the Glass plan bankers elected the members of the Federal Reserve Board; second, currency issue remained in bank control. Bryan wanted the board composed solely of government-appointed officials and, more important, demanded that note issue be solely a function of government. He informed Wilson that the democracy since Jefferson and Jackson, as well as in recent platforms, believed in currency issue as a governmental function. As the bill stood, he could not support it and could not ask his followers to do so either.

In early June Wilson had to decide between the conservative Glass-Willis bill, which would have banker support, and the main points of the Bryan group. So on June 11, 1913, he called in the man whose economic views he trusted and respected most, Louis Brandeis, who by this time distrusted the big banking houses almost to the point of obsession. He only recently had said that "we have no place in American democracy for the money king, not even for the merchant prince. We are confronted in the twentieth century, as we were in the nineteenth century, with an irreconcilable conflict. Our democracy cannot endure half free and half slave. The essence of the trust is a combination of the capitalist, by the capitalist, and for the capitalist."

Brandeis convinced the president not only of the justness of Bryan's arguments in light of Democratic platform pledges but also of their correctness. Even if the Federal Reserve notes should be backed by commercial paper, the currency had to remain exclusively a function of the government. As for banker control: "the American people will not be content to have the discretion necessarily involved vested in a Board composed wholly or in part of bankers; for their judgment may be biased by private interest or affiliations." To bolster these views, Brandeis sounded a dire note on the conflict "between the policies of the Administration and the desires of the financiers and of big business," a conflict he termed "irreconcilable" and in which concessions, in the end, would prove futile.

A monopoly did not exist insofar as one bank or even a few firms had total control over the country's money and credit. But the system as it existed created a pyramid in which small country banks deposited their reserves in larger city banks, which in turn redeposited the money in the major New York, Boston, and Chicago banks. As a result, millions of dollars drawn in from all over the country were at the disposal of a few large banks. Only they were able to provide the huge loans needed by the nation's growing industries, and men like J. P. Morgan and George F. Baker of New York's National City Bank, who, together with their allies, controlled more than $22 billion, exercised enormous influence in American industry. They placed men of their own choosing on the boards of U.S. Steel, General Foods, the New York Central Railroad, and other giant firms. Although Brandeis may have been incorrect in describing American banking as a trust, it was true that a handful of financiers, using other people's money, wielded great and potentially dangerous power. From the reformers' viewpoint this power had to be controlled, and the nature of the banking system required an active role by the government.

On June 18 Wilson summoned his chief advisers to the White House and informed them that he had decided to insist upon exclusive government control of the reserve system and on making its notes government obligations. Bryan was ecstatic and in a public letter declared it a bill "written from the standpoint of the people rather than from the standpoint of the financiers." The government issue provisions, he said, fulfilled Democratic platform principles. With the conservatives and Bryanites reconciled, the president proposed the bill to Congress on June 23 and, despite strong attacks from the banking community, engineered it through Congress and signed it into law before the year ended. In retrospect, it was the most constructive piece of legislation enacted in the Wilson administration.

Imperfect in many details, the bill nevertheless struck that careful balance between private control and public supervision that Wilson and Brandeis so idealized. In a very short time it won the approval of the bankers, especially of the smaller country banks now released from liege to Wall Street. The extreme radicals, however, condemned it. LaFollette denounced it as a "big bankers bill," legalizing the money trust, a charge echoed by Senator Joseph H. Bristow of Kansas and

Representative Charles A. Lindbergh of Minnesota. These critics failed to understand Wilsonian reform or the philosophy of its chief architect.

The basically conservative New Freedom looked not to remold society in a new form but to return to an idyllic (and mythical) past in which the various economic groups of the country existed in nearly perfect harmony. To the extent that it favored popular democracy against a wealthy elite it was progressive, but its liberalism was of the nineteenth-century laissez-faire type, which called for minimal government regulation. Wilson's dilemma was how to combat big business without big government. The Brandeisian approach of government establishing and then regulating a competitive condition rather than regulating business apparently solved the president's anguish. Both Wilson and Brandeis feared letting government go too far. Eventually big government came, and it is ironic that under Wilson the country first experienced both the evils and the benefits of Leviathan. But in December 1913, looking over their handiwork, the two men were satisfied that they had struck their sought-for balance.

The fact that the Wilsonian system broke down at the end of the 1920s does not mean that it was the wrong solution; the president and his chief advisers did not anticipate the extreme pressures of speculative fever and then depression which brought the country's economy and the banking system nearly to a standstill. The progressives rather naively believed that once a solution had been implemented, like a well-designed machine it would run practically forever with only minor adjustments. Franklin Roosevelt and the New Deal had to make major changes in the Federal Reserve System, but the basic structure remained that created by the Wilsonians.

When it became clear that the Federal Reserve bill would pass, Wilson and his administration turned to the problem of what legislation to propose next. Several members of the cabinet urged the president to pause and allow the business community to adjust to the new currency and tariff laws. Secretary of Agriculture David Houston advised Wilson "to make haste slowly," a sentiment shared by several government officials. The sage and respected Major Henry L. Higginson informed the president "that in every direction business is very dull and prospects are discouraging. . . . People are afraid to undertake anything, and are afraid to invest. . . . If from now on for a couple of years we heard nothing about attacking the trusts or pushing government control in any way until we see how the government controlled the banking system of the country, people might take courage and go on."

William Jennings Bryan, however, urged Wilson to fulfill the Democratic pledges on the trusts. From Boston Brandeis advised the president to "Be Bold!" Antitrust legislation was essential to complete the New Freedom and also to "satisfy the demands of the very large number of progressive Democrats and the near Democrats who are already beginning to express some doubts" regarding the administration's courage. The business depression "cannot be ended or lessened by any course which the administration may take. . . . The fearless course is the wise one."

Wilson's views on the subject were still fairly clear, straightforward, and naive: prevent monopoly by punishment of personal guilt. All this was simple enough to say, but Wilson did not know how to do it and never set forth any clear-cut program, except for a strong enforcement of the Sherman Act's criminal provisions. The "moral fire" of righteousness, he believed, should be the instrument of national policy. And in 1914 most Americans still believed that moral principles applied with equal success and certainty to all fields — literature and art, politics and business.

If Wilson approached the trust problem in the role of political moralist, Brandeis came in the garb of social and economic engineer, one who had learned to suspect the greedy nature of economic man. Before congressional hearings he maintained that any real effectiveness of antitrust measures would never be brought out through criminal proceedings; he saw no hope that searing the monopolists' "alleged consciences" would produce any results at all. The proper method would be to decide on the desired goals and then frame just laws which reasonable people would follow. More than twenty years before he met Woodrow Wilson, Brandeis had argued that "no regulation can be enforced which is not reasonable."

Both Brandeis and Wilson argued that democracy could not continue if the economic fate of the nation rested in the hands of an oligopoly. Brandeis, just as interested as the president in keeping open the doors of opportunity to a rising middle class, went further in his determination to save even the wealthy from their own folly. "It is certain," he once said, "that among a free people every excess of capital must in time be repaid by the excessive demands of those who have not the capital." It would be to the advantage of the capitalists to set up reasonable limits and end injustices.

To Brandeis a trust was more than just a political danger; its very size menaced the actual framework of society. Where Wilson argued that bigness in itself was not bad, only its abuses, Brandeis saw bigness itself as the major threat. Too great a concentration of economic power was a social, economic, and political menace to a free society; a business could be efficient only up to a certain size beyond which bigness caused inefficiency; trusts could never stand up to smaller units in a free and truly competitive marketplace; proper rules regulating competition could ensure such conditions; competition was the atmosphere a free society breathes.

The original memorandum Brandeis prepared in 1912 had spelled out a four-point program: first, remove the uncertainties and vagaries of the Sherman Act; second, facilitate the enforcement of the law by the courts; next, create a board or commission to aid in administering the law; and finally, allow trade agreements, subject to the commission's review, to stand if not in violation of competitive rules.

On January 20, 1914, Wilson delivered a special message to Congress on the "great question" of trusts and monopolies. In moderate terms he suggested that "the antagonism between business and government is over," and the time was ripe to proceed with a sensible program — a program representing the "best business judgment in America." He proposed outlawing interlocking directorates in great corporations; allowing the Interstate Commerce Commission power to supervise capital financing and securities issuance by the railroads; setting up a federal commission that would provide businessmen with "the advice, the definite guidance, and information" they needed but would not have the power to "make terms with monopoly or . . . assume control of business"; establishing penalties for individuals guilty of malpractices; and he suggested that any facts or judgments decided upon in government suits would not have to be reproven in suits by private individuals to recover damages. On reading the speech over, Brandeis remarked to his brother that the president "has paved the way for about all I have asked for and some of the provisions specifically are what I got into his mind at my first interview."

For the next few months Brandeis found himself frantically busy in Washington, tied up both in the Interstate Commerce Commission's hearings on railroad rates and in trying to get the president's antitrust program strengthened and enacted. The more radical progressives had been disappointed by Wilson's message, and they hoped that the program could be modified before passage. Samuel Untermyer complained that the proposed bills were "lamentably weak and ineffective. . . . [The] so-called Trade Commission Bill is nothing more at present than a Bureau of Information with little more than the existing Bureau of Corporations and with vastly added expense." He begged Colonel House to get Brandeis in to redraw the measure. House agreed, and when he forwarded Untermyer's letter to Wilson, he urged him "to put Gregory and Brandeis on this job with the Attorney-General to act as advisor." The president took up the suggestion with alacrity, writing to Congressman Adamson that since Brandeis was in Washington, he should appear before the House committee holding hearings on the Clayton and Trade Commission bills. Brandeis reluctantly agreed, although he much preferred to continue the intricate work on railroad rate schedules before the ICC, and for several days in mid-February he testified before the House Judiciary Committee.

Brandeis himself was not completely happy with all the proposed measures, and on February 22 he sent Attorney General James McReynolds a detailed letter suggesting ways of strengthening the antitrust law. Brandeis in particular wanted the section dealing with interlocking directorates made foolproof. He had urged the House committee to realize the importance of this idea and lectured them on the dangers: "The principle that no man can serve two masters . . . is fundamental, and when a man undertakes to serve two corporations that are dealing with one another there is always the danger that the unethical relation may result in loss . . . generally to the public through lessened efficiency." He reminded McReynolds that the prohibition against interlocking directorates had been omitted from the Federal Reserve Act on the pledge that it would be included in antitrust legislation, and that such a clause would "stop the concentration of money power." On March 1 Brandeis closeted himself with the attorney general and his advisers for the better part of the day, going over all the parts of the program. Two weeks later Congressman Clayton agreed to the insertion of a strong prohibition and requested Brandeis to draft the measure. A Trade Commission bill as well as the Clayton bill passed the House on June 5. But once the bills reached the Senate, pressures built up to change them, pressures based on the belief that the bills were unrealistic, ineffective, and totally unworkable.

The provision on individual guilt, so dear to Wilson's heart, frightened both large and small businessmen. After the mad scramble of unrestrained and cutthroat competition of the Gilded Age, American businessmen had begun to look for methods that would avoid not only destructive excesses but also governmental regulation. The groundwork for the great trade association activities of the 1920s was being worked out at this time, and the Clayton antitrust bill threatened to halt this new cooperation. Conceivably, a zealot in the attorney general's office could interpret the law so as to reward any act of cooperation with a fine, a jail sentence, or both. In addition, many progressives as well as businessmen denied the possibility of statutorily defining all practices in restraint of trade. Brandeis himself admitted the great difficulty of trying to define in advance all illicit methods of competition. George Rublee, a New York lawyer who worked with Brandeis on the legislation, later recalled the fears that in attempting to be too specific the Clayton Act would leave open the doors to every sort of evasion American ingenuity could develop. Critics of the program came to prefer a stronger trade commission, with discretionary powers, to enforce the legislative wishes as defined in general but comprehensive terms. Rather than attempt to list all illegal practices, they argued, outlaw all such practices in general terms and let the commission decide upon specifics. Wilson, upset and confused by the criticism, nonetheless recognized the validity of the arguments; but he hesitated, his old fears against governmental regulation still strong.

At this time Brandeis, almost involuntarily, acted decisively to alter the president's thinking. Rublee and Congressman Raymond B. Stevens of New Hampshire both believed in a strong trade commission, and they drew up a bill incorporating this idea. Brandeis himself, during the winter and spring of 1914, gave only cursory thought to the problem because of the ICC railroad investigation. Both Stevens and Rublee believed that Brandeis opposed the strong commission they wanted and hesitated to discuss the matter with him. Finally, however, they got Senator Henry Hollis to make an appointment for them with the president on June 10, and at the last moment they asked Brandeis to go along. Rublee said he knew that Brandeis did not approve of their ideas, but if he went with them, Wilson would listen to their proposals. Brandeis agreed, and after Rublee made the presentation, the president asked the Boston lawyer what he thought. Brandeis then turned on all his persuasive charm and, much to everyone's surprise, proceeded to tell the president why he should support the proposal. Wilson, who had already seen the Stevens bill, needed only the assurance that he was not surrendering any of the New Freedom principles. Brandeis provided the assurance he needed.

Brandeis, like Wilson, originally opposed such a commission, which smacked so much of Roosevelt's New Nationalism. But Brandeis had gradually come to believe that it would be impossible to define statutorily all possible violations and that it would be better to lay down legislative guidelines that could then be expanded by a regulatory agency. At Wilson's behest Brandeis now went to see several senators to apprise them of the situation, and he appeared before the Senate Interstate Commerce Committee later in the month. In answer to a direct question on the Stevens bill's parentage, he admitted that he, Rublee, and Stevens had worked it up into its final form. Soon afterward, with the aid of White House pressure and a few modifications in the Clayton bill, both the antitrust and the Federal Trade Commission proposals became law. Their enactment brought the original New Freedom to an end. Shortly afterward war erupted in Europe, and a new cause claimed Brandeis's attention.

V

Zionism

Brandeis did not join the Zionists until 1912, nor did he take any active role until 1914. Yet once involved, Brandeis's devotion to the re-creation of a Jewish homeland in Palestine never wavered. He gave more of his fortune and energy to Zionism than to any other of his causes, and in doing so he completely reshaped the movement in America.

The dream of restoration to their promised land had begun the moment the Jews were defeated in the Roman wars and exiled from Palestine in the second century. For most of the following 1800 years redemption of the land was tied to another dream, the messianic "end of days." For traditional Jews this exile was part of God's great plan, in which he had punished the Jewish people for breaking its covenant with him. But God had also promised to redeem his people, and for centuries Jews had prayed for a messenger to free them from oppression and return them to their holy land. Not until the nineteenth century did Jewish thinkers begin to contemplate the possibility that people could bring about their own redemption, that the Jewish people did not have to wait for the Messiah to free them from persecution and reclaim their ancient heritage.

Such ideas found a fertile ground in the 1880s and 1890s. The rising tide of secular nationalism, a revival of Hebrew letters and literature, and the intolerable conditions fostered by official anti-Semitism in Russia led thousands of Jews to join the *Hibbat Zion* (love of Zion) movement. The first modern Jewish pioneers in Palestine founded the settlements at Rishon L'Tziyon and G'dera, proving that Jews could forsake the European ghettos. But the fullest expression of modern Zionism came from an assimilated Austrian Jew, Theodor Herzl, who knew little of Jewish learning and nothing of the *Hibbat Zion*. Appalled by the hatred he witnessed at the Dreyfus trial in Paris, Herzl set out in his tract *The Jewish State* the basic theses that until the Jews had a home of their own, they would not be free from the tyrannies of a prejudiced world; and that they could and would establish this homeland by their own labors in Palestine. In 1897 at the First Zionist Congress Herzl brought into being the organization that would oversee this reclamation, and before his death in 1904 the basic institutions which would ultimately make Zionism work had been created.

Although Zionism found some adherents in the United States, for the most part American Jews either ignored the movement or dismissed it contemptuously. Jews had found a new Zion in America, a land that welcomed immigrants and paid little attention to their religion. Here were no officially imposed ghettos or quotas but a freedom that allowed Jewish immigrants to prosper freely. America lacked the feudal legacies of class structure and prejudice, which had fostered and sustained anti-Semitism in Europe.

The Jewish immigrants from Eastern Europe did not forsake Zion so much as submerge their dreams of it. In the United States they devoted almost every waking minute to eking out a living for their families. Beyond that they wanted desperately to stop being greenhorns, and both the established German-Jewish aristocracy as well as most native American leaders told them that true Americanism required a single and undeviating loyalty to the United States. Zionism, especially in Reform eyes, led to a divided loyalty and thus to an inferior Americanism. Until August 1914 the overwhelming majority of American Jews turned their backs on Zionism; only when the horrors of war overran European Jewry did American Jews rediscover the depth of their own ethnic ties and the extent of a long-hidden love of Zion.

The war totally disrupted the World Zionist Organization, which for all practical purposes ceased to function. Berlin housed the main headquarters, but the Jewish Colonial Trust, the organization's bank, operated out of London; Palestinian colonies lay under Turkish rule, but many of the settlers had retained Russian citizenship. The settlements' economy depended upon the export of wine and citrus to Europe, but embargoes virtually shut down normal trade. Members of the Zionist executive, scattered across the continent, could not meet, while the Jewish communities of Eastern Europe, the center of Zionist ferment, lay in the middle of the heaviest fighting between Germany and Russia. In this chaos the Jews and Zionists of Europe turned to the only major community in the world untouched by the conflagration, and they sought not only material relief but guidance and leadership as well.

One member of the Zionist executive, Shmarya Levin, had just completed an American tour when war broke out, and he took the lead in trying to get the various Zionist groups to cooperate in raising relief money for Jews of Europe and Palestine. Levin realized that more established non-Zionist bodies like the American Jewish Committee would be active in this area, but he hoped that the Zionists might secure increased visibility and support within the community. To this end Levin called an emergency meeting in New York for August 30, 1914. Among those receiving invitations to the conference at the Hotel Marseilles, Louis Brandeis probably had had the least exposure to or involvement with the Zionist movement. Yet at the urging of Jacob deHaas, Brandeis agreed to accept the chairmanship of a temporary relief committee. Of all those who planned to attend, only Brandeis's name would have been recognized by many Americans. If the Zionists wanted to raise money, they needed a leader who was himself well-to-do and who had access to other wealthy men. As deHaas later noted, no one really expected Brandeis to take this committee leadership seriously.

Brandeis accepted the nomination of the Provisional Executive Committee for General Zionist Affairs and briefly talked about the plight of Jews in the war-afflicted areas. He then announced the establishment of an Emergency Fund and began the subscription with a donation of $1000 to which Nathan Straus added another $5000. So far everything had gone according to expectations: a relief fund had been inaugurated with a well-known personality to head it, and now they would let him get some of his rich friends to give more. Then the script suddenly changed. Brandeis, pleading his ignorance of the many organizations represented, asked the assembly to stay on and meet with him that evening and the following day. He needed to know more about them, their leaders, their memberships, their administrative arrangements. For the next day and a half Brandeis sat patiently in a crowded hotel suite, absorbing fact after fact about Zionism and Jewish life in America, occasionally asking a question or repeating a strange-sounding Hebrew or Yiddish name. When he finally adjourned the meeting late on August 31, his orderly mind might well have been reeling from the realization that nearly all the groups present had poor organization, modest enrollments, minuscule financial resources, and very, very few people ready to do real work. But the shock to the men and women representing American Zionism was immeasurably greater; the extraordinary conference had brought them not a figurehead but a man who had the ability, determination, and reputation to be their leader, and who intended to do just that. The Hotel Marseilles meeting marked a turning point not only in the life of Louis Brandeis but in the fortunes of American Zionism as well.

Little in Brandeis's family background, or even in the first five decades of his life, explained his relatively sudden interest and passionate involvement in Zionism. His association with Judaism remained tenuous. He never joined a synagogue or any fraternal group, and while never denying his Jewish ancestry, neither did he advertise it. He made a number of donations to various Jewish charities, but he gave equal or greater amounts to non-Jewish causes. Those who knew him well in those days could not recall any overt evidence of Jewish identification on his part. His letters and speeches rarely mentioned religion, and when he sprinkled quotations among his writings, he invariably went to Shakespeare, Goethe, and the Greeks, hardly ever to the Bible. Although he had a number of Jewish clients, Brandeis did not know many Jews, and these few were mostly like himself — American-born, assimilated, and ignorant of the rich culture of Eastern European Jewry. If they practiced any formal religion, it was usually in the Reform mode; Brandeis himself had been and would remain totally nonobservant.

Louis Brandeis came to Zionism, as he himself said many times, through Americanism, and his experiences and attitudes — not his marginal Jewishness — reshaped Zionism in America. His approach to the Jewish problem remarkably resembled his approach to the secular problems confronting industrial America. Brandeis and the men and women he attracted to the movement had a clear and firm commitment to American ideas and democratic principles. They objected to anti-Semitism not from personal suffering but because it offended their sense of decency. Zionism, which reflected so many of the progressive ideals, became for many of them a reform movement, akin to women's suffrage or factory legislation. This outlook on Zionism, as a reform to solve the Jewish problem, provided the strength — and the weakness — of their leadership.

Brandeis faced three great tasks on assuming the Zionist leadership, and his success or failure in handling them would determine whether Zionism emerged as a potent force in American Jewish life or continued an anemic existence, of small consequence to all but the devoted few. He had to reorganize Zionist forces into an effective form; he had to identify specific projects that would attract those who shared only a marginal interest in Zionism; finally, and most important, he had to redefine Zionist assumptions to fit the needs of American as well as Jewish society.

As late as 1910 Brandeis shared the fears of many Americans that the masses of new immigrants, Jewish as well as non-Jewish, would cling too tenaciously to their Old World loyalties. In 1905, at ceremonies marking the 250th anniversary of the Jewish presence in America, Brandeis had echoed Theodore Roosevelt's dictum that America had no room for "hyphenated" Americans. "There is room here for men of any race, of any creed, of any condition in life," he declared, "but not for Protestant-Americans, or Catholic-Americans, or Jewish-Americans, not for German-Americans, Irish-Americans, or Russian-Americans. This country demands that its sons and daughters whatever their race — however intense or diverse their religious connections — be politically merely American citizens." Nothing that Brandeis said would have differentiated him from aristocratic German-American Jews like Jacob Schiff or Louis Marshall, who condemned Zionism as antithetical to true Americanism.

Brandeis's involvement in the New York garment strike altered his attitudes toward the Russian immigrants, a group he admittedly knew little about. This contact, as he testified, led him to understand for the first time the Jewish experience and culture. He saw, however, not religious ritual and dogma but a reflection of those very traits that his New England background had made dear — democracy, social justice, and individuality tempered by group responsibility. "I now saw the true democracy of my people, their idealistic inclinations and their love of liberty and freedom." Brandeis had discovered, as would many progressives, that diversity need not be detrimental in a democratic society, provided different groups subscribed to a common set of ethical and social principles. In his speeches Brandeis began to develop those ideas that would later be termed "cultural pluralism."

By interpreting Jewish-Zionist idealism as complementary and supportive of American democracy, Brandeis undercut the claim that Zionism was inconsistent with or antithetical to Americanism. "America's fundamental law seeks to make real the brotherhood of man. That brotherhood became the Jews' fundamental law more than twenty-five hundred years ago. America's twentieth-century demand is for social justice. That has been the Jews' striving ages-long." Addressing the 1915

Zionist convention in Boston, he proclaimed: "The highest Jewish ideals are essentially American in a very important particular. It is Democracy that Zionism represents. It is Social Justice which Zionism represents, and every bit of that is the American ideals of the twentieth-century." The ideals and desire for liberty that had marked the earliest Americans and had shaped the nation's destiny now stood reborn in a movement to allow the Jews to live in freedom. As he learned about the Jewish heritage, he began to see that "Jews were by reason of their traditions and their character peculiarly fitted for the attainment of American ideals." This observation led him to make the ultimate link, not only bridging Zionism and Americanism but welding the two together: *To be good Americans, we must be better Jews, and to be better Jews, we must become Zionist.*

Decades of anti-Zionist argument could not, of course, be swept away with the assertion that America demanded its Jews become Zionists, even when it came from such an eminent personality, so Brandeis carefully responded to the main concerns of dual loyalty and the relation of American Jews to a Palestinian homeland. But he went beyond just denying charges, and rather than merely defending Zionism, he called for Jews to be openly proud of its goals and accomplishments.

From the start anti-Zionists had attacked the movement as fostering divided loyalties. One could not be fully patriotic to America, they asserted, if one supported a Jewish homeland somewhere else. Such statements on the surface seemed reasonable enough, and Brandeis himself had argued that one could not serve two masters at the same time. Such logic, however, assumed that the two goals had to be in conflict, that one could not support Zionism because it would weaken one's Americanism. Brandeis seized upon this assumption and labeled it false. "Multiple loyalties are objectionable only if they are inconsistent," he maintained, but the American political system clearly proved that such need not be the case. "A man is a better citizen of the United States for being loyal to his family, and to his profession or trade; for being loyal to his college or lodge." The true loyalty of an American lay not in a superficial allegiance to the symbols of a country but in a deeper, heartfelt commitment to the principles that the nation represented. One believed in freedom, justice, and democracy not just in one place or for one group but everywhere and for all people, and in working for these goals, one evidenced a truer depth of feeling. "Every Irish-American who contributed toward advancing home rule was a better man and a better American for the sacrifices he made," Brandeis asserted, and the same would be said of the Jews. By supporting a free and democratic homeland for their brethren in Palestine, they would be giving the best possible proof of their loyalty to America.

A Palestinian homeland, moreover, would help Jews achieve the sense of pride and identification that other national groups enjoyed, and which enlarged their contribution to American society. As important as proving that Palestine was capable of becoming a Jewish homeland was the need to prove "that the modern Jew is fit for Palestine." After centuries of impoverished city dwelling, four decades of labor in Palestine now stood as testimony to the courage of the Jewish people. Moreover, the Holy Land would serve as a spiritual center to inspire Jews in the rest of the world. Time and again Brandeis referred to the *idealism* of Zionism, to its tone of moral uplift. He reminded his audiences that even though Palestine would always be a tiny country, it had already inspired three of the world's great religions. "The only thing of real value in life is the ideal," he asserted, and the Zionist movement brought out the best in the Jewish people. Striving for an ideal made people better than they thought they were, and he frequently quoted Herzl: *"Wenn ihr es wollt, ist es Kein Maerschen"* — If you will it, it is not a dream.

Neither Brandeis's Zionist ideology nor his concept of Americanism was new, but his unique contribution to Jewish life in America lay in his synthesis of the two. Thoroughly American in spirit, his imagination had been captured by a vision of a homeland where a people he hardly knew could live freely, a vision popularized by another assimilated Jew,

Theodor Herzl, who had also discovered his Jewishness late in life. Brandeis saw Palestine as a small country free from the "curse of bigness," one that could experiment in enlarging the bounds of freedom and social justice, much as a state within the United States could serve as a laboratory for legislative experimentation. He assumed from the start that the Jewish homeland would be a democracy, with men and women equal partners in building a free society; revealingly, he once wrote that the ideals he had for America "should also prevail in the Jewish State."

In essence Zionism represented a reawakening of the Jewish spirit, a revival of a long-dormant nationalism. It also marked the beginning of a rebellion in which Jews for the first time in eighteen centuries refused to knuckle under to repression. This pride, this idealism, this effort to shape one's own destiny appealed not only to Brandeis but to other progressives as well. The element of protest fit into the overall reform temperament and won Zionism a sympathetic response in the progressive ranks. This sentiment brought into the movement Jewish men and women who, with few exceptions, had had little contact with either Zionism or Jewish communal life. When Shmaryahu Levin joyously reported to the Actions Committee in 1915 that a "new Zionism" had developed in the United States, he termed its leaders "men of earnestness and of character, who demand logical completeness in the movements with which they affiliate, who devote themselves full-heartedly to the movement of which they are part." This new leadership dominated American Zionism from 1914 to 1921 and would later return to power in the 1930s. Like Brandeis, who personally recruited many of them, they shared a fundamental commitment to American ideals, and they had won their reputation in fields uninvolved with Judaism. United States Circuit Court Judge Julian W. Mack, for example, espoused the idea of cultural pluralism in a democratic society and, like Brandeis, worked for a living law in developing the juvenile court program. Rabbi Stephen S. Wise belonged to that small group of Reform rabbis who did not see Zionism as inconsistent with modern Judaism, and beyond that he was an active participant in several progressive crusades. Harvard Law Professor Felix Frankfurter did not hold formal office, but from 1914 to 1919 he played an active role in Zionist affairs. Frankfurter came as close as any man to being Brandeis's disciple, but although they shared many reform and legal interests, Frankfurter's Zionist work waned after 1921. Henrietta Szold, the founder of Hadassah (the American women's Zionist organization) discovered a strong supporter in Brandeis, who endorsed Hadassah's program of practical health care in Palestine.

Brandeis's call for members brought in more than leaders and those willing to lend their names to a cause; it also led to the enrollment of tens of thousands of American Jews who had previously ignored Zionism. At the 1914 convention the Federation of American Zionists (FAZ) claimed a membership of little more than 12,000; by 1919 the figure stood at over 176,000, with thousands of others associated with the various religious or labor Zionist groups. This increased membership growing out of the war crisis made possible a growth in the budget as well as the reorganization of the FAZ into the Zionist Organization of America.

In all his work Brandeis stood by the motto: "Men! Money! Discipline!" Nothing could be done without members, and Brandeis hammered home this demand wherever he went. "Organize! Organize! Organize! until every Jew in America must stand up and be counted — counted with us — or prove himself, wittingly, of the few who are against their own people." Members provided workers who would spread Zionist propaganda. Members provided funds for the Palestinian colonies. Members provided the essential resources that made possible the assumption of new projects and responsibilities.

To secure these members, the Provisional Committee adopted a number of stratagems. Brandeis and others went on speaking tours to appeal for new members. Whenever people asked how they could help, the answer invariably came back to enroll as a member and then bring in others.

"Every one of you should consider himself an organizer, and no day should elapse without some addition to the number of members in the local organization." Brandeis, never content with merely preaching to others, rigorously followed his own orders and talked of Zionism to nearly all the Jewish reformers he knew. After several weeks of importuning by Brandeis and Frankfurter, Eugene Meyer, Jr., finally threw up his hands and consented to head the newly formed University Zionist Association. Mary Fels, Louis Kirstein, Nathan Straus, and others also acceded to such personal suasion.

Although the leadership had access to names, real growth in membership had to occur on the local level. Here the organizational methods of the Brandeis group contrasted vividly with the haphazard and random recruitment of the FAZ. In addition to constant encouragement, the leadership instituted procedures to promote orderly yet rapid growth and also established new organizations to appeal to those groups previously untouched by Zionism. At the lowest level, members received instructions in private gatherings and home parties, with local organizations responsible for providing speakers or demonstrations. At the next level, local groups were assigned specific quotas, with target dates by which to meet these goals. A speakers bureau set up by the Provisional Committee supplied Zionist orators, both in English and in Yiddish, to the mass rallies run by the local societies, with immediate follow-ups to see how effective their efforts had been. Sometimes the targets appeared unrealistic. When the Zionists held their 1915 convention in Boston, Brandeis appealed to the Chelsea society to "set an example of Jewish unity, not only to America, but to the whole world . . . by enrolling as a member of the Chelsea Zionist Society every adult male Jew in the city, and by enrolling every member of his family as a shekel payer."

The weekly and monthly reports by the constituent societies were not for show or to make local committees believe that someone back at headquarters was watching. Under the direction of Jacob deHaas the office committee had begun accumulating a master card index. Every Jew in America who paid the membership fee had his or her name on a card, as did those who contributed to any of the Zionist-affiliated funds. This index became the starting point for intensive recruiting campaigns and ultimately consisted of over a half million names. For the first time the Zionists had reliable information on its membership and realistic data from which to seek new members. The method had been utilized by nearly all progressive groups and reflected the impulse for orderliness that characterized much of the reform mood at this time. That the FAZ had made practically no efforts to organize its recruitment into some manageable form indicated how far it had stood from the mainstream of American life.

The majority of American Jews in 1914 claimed Eastern European origin, with many of them but recently arrived from Russia, Poland, or parts of the Austro-Hungarian Empire. They still worked in factories or small shops, and until the war socialist ideology concerned them far more than Zionism. They had not forgotten Zion — nor could they have done so if they had wished; the entire Jewish milieu of Eastern Europe, with its traditions, messianic fervor, and love of the Holy Land, could not be thrown off on a boat trip. Many still had relatives in the old country affected by the war, and even those with small means wanted to help their brethren. When the Zionists established a relief fund, and Brandeis declared Zionism and Americanism compatible, he not only provided the recent immigrants with a means to help their relatives but also unleashed long-buried emotions.

Brandeis, however, did more than just awaken their latent love for Zion; he also brought to the surface their simmering resentment against the established German-Jewish elite, especially the American Jewish Committee (AJC) of Jacob Schiff and Louis Marshall. More than just Zionism separated the *yahudim* (the uptown German Jews) from the *yidden* (the downtown immigrants from Eastern Europe). The German aristocrats looked down at the less acculturated newcomers and were often patronizing in their dealings with them. The established Jews like Marshall, Schiff, Warburg, Guggenheim, and Strauss had given millions for the aid of their fellow Jews and had created many of the great philanthropic agencies for their welfare. But they had done so with an air of superiority; they claimed to know best what the immigrants needed, and the unspoken price of their aid was submission to their leadership. They also had definite ideas about how the immigrants should go about becoming Americans, and this did not include support of Jewish nationalism, which Schiff and his peers viewed as undermining a true Americanism.

From the start Brandeis had recognized that at some time he would have to tackle the power of the American Jewish Committee. Marshall had been less than thrilled when the Zionists started a relief fund of their own rather than supporting the Committee's program. Though the Zionists did operate a successful transfer fund, in which American Jews could send money to relatives and friends in Europe, it soon became apparent that they had no access to the wealthier Jews other than Nathan Strauss of Macy's. The Provisional Committee received thousands of small contributions, all helpful in building membership, but Jacob Schiff and his friends, many of whom belonged to the American Jewish Committee, could through one donation surpass the Zionist sums. The logic of the situation called for a unified effort, and since the big givers supported the Committee, the Joint Distribution Committee, as the combined operation became known, came under the American Jewish Committee's sway.

The vehicle Brandeis ultimately chose to challenge the aristocracy reflected the most progressive of causes, democracy. The downtown Jews referred to the Committee members as *shtadlonim,* or court Jews, who in Europe had often interceded with authorities by bribing government officials to protect Jews. The Committee's methods — quiet conferences with government leaders — had often brought results, but they did smack of an autocracy which did things *for* rather than *with* the masses, of an air of superiority and condescension. The immigrants did not so much fail to appreciate what the Schiffs and Warburgs did for them as object to the lack of their own participation. If America meant anything to the newcomers from Eastern Europe, it meant democracy.

For several years many Jewish leaders had been calling for the creation of a representative body of all American Jewish groups. The American Jewish Committee had steadfastly opposed such a new agency, arrogating unto itself the right to speak for American Jewry. Brandeis, both for philosophical and political reasons, adopted the cause of an American Jewish congress as his own. On principle he opposed the elitism of the Committee, an attitude all too reminiscent of the Brahmins he had been fighting for fifteen years. Brandeis could be inflexible and even dogmatic at times, but he had a deep devotion to democracy in practice as well as in theory. The Committee's methods offended him as going against the basic premises of American life. Politically he recognized that during a war against Prussian autocracy, a call for a democratic congress would carry great emotional appeal. It would be very difficult for the American Jewish Committee to claim that its closed membership, its secret maneuverings and its aristocratic mentality represented the American ideal. Brandeis's vehicle for his own and the Zionist leadership would be a fight on grounds that the Committee had always claimed as its own, a "true Americanism."

The Zionist call for a representative congress brought immediate denunciations from Committee leaders. Jacob Schiff denounced Brandeis and his colleagues for this irresponsible action, which had now called the loyalty of all American Jewry into question. "With the actual holding of the proposed Congress," he warned, "the coming of political anti-Semitism into this land will be only a question of time. There is no room in the United States for any other Congress upon national lines, except the American Congress." Louis Marshall joined in the attack upon "blatant and flamboyant orators" who inflicted such great damage on their fellow Jews. From the time the

Provisional Executive Committee first broached the idea in 1914, the American Jewish Committee and its leaders tried to denigrate the proposal, insisting that the better elements among American Jews knew best how to handle the community's affairs.

Although the proposal for a congress had been put forward several times in the past, it now had a sponsorship that, from its experience in progressive reform, knew how to prepare for battle. It also had a pressing reason for existence, the protection of Jewish rights in Europe after the war. By mid 1915 a Congress Organizing Committee had been formed, representing more than a score of Jewish groups, all of which had downtown constituencies. While Brandeis directed the overall strategy, he differed with a number of his followers, especially Stephen Wise and Louis Lipsky, over how hard to push the battle. He recognized, as did Louis Marshall, that too complete a victory for either side would split the community. If the American Jewish Committee defeated the congress, it would further alienate the new immigrants; on the other hand, a congress without the *yahudim* could not claim real representation of American Jewry. Even as the firebrands on both sides fought back and forth, Brandeis and Marshall tried to keep open some room for maneuvering, some path for compromise.

Finally, the Committee overplayed its hand. It offered as a compromise a pre-preliminary meeting whose composition it would determine. The proposed distribution of representatives bore no relation at all to the size of their groups but reflected the Committee's view of who the better elements in the community were. The publication of this ludicrous proposal only confirmed the popular image of the American Jewish Committee as an elitist and authoritarian body, and Brandeis now turned loose the Congress Organizing Committee, declaring that no concessions would be made to autocracy. By the fall of 1915 machinery for the selection of delegates had been put into operation, and the leadership of American Jewry began shifting away from the Committee and toward the Zionists. When Schiff, Marshall, and Cyrus Adler recognized this, they quietly indicated that perhaps the Committee could agree to a congress, provided it met after the war.

This offer posed a serious dilemma for Brandeis. On the one hand, the congress movement now had an energy of its own; to attempt to limit it might cripple the entire program. There were also tactical problems with a congress which would not convene until after the hostilities ended; one prepared for peace in advance of war's end, not after the fighting, and the major purpose of the congress would be to formulate demands for the safety and well-being of European Jewry after the war. On the other side, the American Jewish Committee had a cogent argument when it said that nothing should be done by the Jews that would embarrass the American government, at that time still a neutral power in the war. Beyond that Brandeis saw, if few others did, that the congress fight, the relief work, and the Zionist leadership all devolved upon the same small group of men; he and his colleagues were being pushed to their limits, and if they were to continue the congress drive, something else would have to be abandoned.

To buy time, and also perhaps to force the Committee into offering better terms, Brandeis ordered his staff to increase its pressure for the congress by developing plans for local branches and stepping up its propaganda campaign regarding the democratic nature of the congress. Privately he tried to reason with Committee leaders, to make them see that the immigrants' demand for a congress could not be stopped. In January 1916 at a mass rally in New York, Brandeis made his strongest plea yet for a congress, speaking both of democracy in American Jewish life and the need for protection of Jewish rights overseas. Shortly afterward the Congress Organizing Committee called for a preliminary conference in Philadelphia in late March.

A total of 367 delegates from 83 cities and 28 states attended the Philadelphia meeting, representing 33 national organizations with a combined membership of more than a million Jews. The entire program moved smoothly, a testimony to the organizational skills of Brandeis and other American Jewish leaders who had learned their trade in secular reforms. Even the *American Israelite,* which usually endorsed the Committee position, conceded that the congress movement had gathered more popular support among American Jews than had ever been seen before. Although the Committee boycotted the conference, its success highlighted how alienated it had become from the rest of the community.

Finally the American Jewish Committee faced the inevitable. No one had ever wanted to exclude it from the congress but merely to force it to share power with the masses. This the Committee now agreed to do, albeit reluctantly, and in fact managed through a series of complicated maneuvers to turn defeat into a form of victory. American entry into the war in April 1917 led Wilson to request that the congress postpone its formal meeting until after the hostilities; moreover, the Committee managed to secure a limited agenda, as well as agreement that the congress would function only until it had secured satisfactory guaranties of Jewish rights at a peace conference.

The battle did result, however, in the demise of the American Jewish Committee as the preeminent organization of American Jewish leadership. Unfortunately, the American Jewish Congress never developed into the overarching agency that Brandeis, Wise, and their followers had envisioned, in part because of changing patterns in American Jewish life, patterns that prevented any single organization from securing the level of power once enjoyed by the Committee. In addition, the compromises that Brandeis made to secure the cooperation of the Committee precluded long-range success for the congress. And a major reason Marshall and Adler were able to win these concessions was because in the spring of 1916 nearly all of Brandeis's energies shifted away from the congress movement, as he became the cause célèbre of American progressivism.

VI

The Court Fight

On an otherwise slow Friday toward the end of January 1916, city editors around the country perusing the wire service ticker tapes were suddenly jolted out of their lethargy. Shortly after noon on January 28 a clerk had delivered a brief message from the White House: "To the Senate of the United States. I nominate Louis D. Brandeis of Massachusetts to be Associate Justice of the Supreme Court of the United States."

Ever since George Washington had sent his first nomination to the Senate seeking its advice and consent, such requests had for the most part been honored quickly and with a minimum of fuss; this had been especially true of the honor-laden appointments to the nation's highest tribunal. But when Woodrow Wilson named Brandeis to the Court, he precipitated a four-month battle, which examined in minute detail nearly every facet of the nominee's life and career. Brandeis himself never appeared before the Senate committee weighing his qualifications; this was still the era in which the office sought the man, so that major parties, after their presidential conventions, sent a delegation to the successful candidate to inform him of the decision and secure his assent.

Few episodes in American history shed so much light on their era, for the lineup of supporters and detractors was a clear demarcation of progressives from those opposed to the reform movement. Despite the injection of some religious and social prejudices into the debate, the major issue at all times remained whether or not to admit a radical into the sacrosanct — and conservative — citadel of the law.

In making the nomination, Wilson no doubt took political considerations into account. His plurality in 1912 had been only 6.3 million out of 15 million votes, and any act invariably had political overtones. Moreover, all nominations had to take into account the realities of political life. The late Justice Lamar had been from Georgia, and Southerners might insist that his replacement also come from Dixie. Neither Massachusetts senator, the patrician Henry Cabot Lodge or the conservative John W. Weeks, sympathized with Brandeis's reform outlook; if they chose to exercise senatorial privilege, the entire Senate might turn down the nomination in deference to their request. What most concerned Wilson, however, was the uncertainty surrounding Theodore Roosevelt's plans for 1916. The Bull Moose ticket had drawn over 4 million votes in 1912, and many progressives still found themselves attracted to the leadership of the mercurial T.R. If Roosevelt returned to the Republican party, Wilson would be hard put to portray himself as the progressive candidate. By naming Brandeis, Wilson in one grand gesture took the high ground for himself. All reform groups respected the people's lawyer and recognized the president's courage in naming a man of the people rather than a defender of the corporate status quo to the Court.

Wilson first had to see whether Brandeis would accept the call. After careful consideration, Brandeis accepted. "I am not exactly sure," he wrote his brother, "that I am to be congratulated, but I am glad the President wanted to make the appointment and I am convinced, all things considered, that I ought to accept." Alice Brandeis reflected her husband's ambivalence: "I had some misgivings for Louis has been such a 'free man' all these years but as you suggested — his days of 'knight erranting' must have, in the nature of things, been over before long."

The announcement of January 28, as Wilson had anticipated, stirred up a rumpus. Delighted reformers showered both the president and his nominee with hundreds of congratulatory messages. The *Boston Post,* the *New York World,* and other liberal papers cheered the news. Former Massachusetts Governor David I. Walsh called the nomination "admirable in every way. Mr. Brandeis is a real progressive, with a profound knowledge of the law, and is certain to prove one of the great jurists that has ever sat on the Supreme Bench." Numerous Zionist and labor organizations vigorously applauded the appointment, both for the honor it brought to Brandeis and for the implicit recognition of the justness of their own causes.

Conservatives reacted with shock and horror. The *New York Sun* deplored the appointment of a radical to "the stronghold of sane conservatism, the safeguard of our institutions, the ultimate interpreter of our fundamental law." Former President William Howard Taft, who had vainly hoped that Wilson would "rise above politics" to name him to the bench, declared that "it is one of the deepest wounds I have had as an American and a lover of the Constitution and a believer in progressive conservatism, that such a man as Brandeis could be put on the Court." Brandeis, the *New York Times* complained, "is essentially a contender, a striver after change and reforms. The Supreme Court by its very nature is the conservator of our institutions."

There was also a muted note regarding the nominee's religion. For the cruder bigots the very fact that Brandeis was Jewish was enough reason to bar him from the temple of the law. The *New York Sun,* for its part, complained that Wilson hoped to capture the large Jewish vote in New York through this gross manipulation of patronage. William Taft asserted that he held nothing against Brandeis for being Jewish; rather, the Bostonian was an opportunist who had embraced Judaism and Zionism only to further his own political ambitions. On the whole, however, the religious issue played a minor role, although there is no doubt that many members of the upper-class, Protestant elite felt uncomfortable about a Jew reaching such an exalted position. For his backers Brandeis was a liberal and a reformer, a prophet of a humane law, the type of man the Supreme Court desperately needed; to his opponents Brandeis appeared utterly untrustworthy, a radical and a demagogue to be kept off the nation's highest tribunal at all costs.

Both sides quickly set about preparing their cases to present to the Senate subcommittee appointed to investigate Brandeis's qualifications. Former President Taft and his one-time Attorney General George W. Wickersham began marshaling opposition among the pillars of the American Bar Association. Clarence Barron, publisher of the business-oriented *Wall Street Journal*, unleashed a barrage of charges and innuendos about Brandeis's supposed chicanery as a lawyer. In Boston the Brahmins were determined not to let Brandeis enter the hallowed chambers of the Court, and they counted upon Henry Cabot Lodge, who socially and intellectually detested all that Brandeis stood for, to lead the battle. Lodge, however, was in a quandary. With the passage of the Seventeenth Amendment he would no longer be returned to the Senate by a conservative state legislature but would have to run for the office in 1916. Among the "great unwashed" who regrettably could now vote directly for their senators, Brandeis was a hero and Lodge had no desire to alienate those whose ballots he would need. To his correspondents Lodge urged that the lawyers in the Senate would gladly listen to their peers; let the bar associations testify to Brandeis's lack of character and his unfitness for the bench. In letter after letter Lodge called upon those who had influence and prestige to gather their forces and make clear that people of quality had no faith in Brandeis's integrity.

"People of quality," especially in Boston, eagerly responded to Lodge's appeal. A. Lawrence Lowell, president of Harvard, reflected on the problem that Boston's leaders had in trying to fight the appointment: "Are we," Lowell asked, "to put on our Supreme Bench a man whose reputation for integrity is not unimpeachable? It is difficult — perhaps impossible — to get direct evidence of any act of Brandeis that is, strictly speaking, dishonest; and yet a man who is believed by all the better part of the bar to be unscrupulous ought not to be a member of the highest court of the nation." Lowell's analysis accurately foretold the course of the four-month attack on Brandeis: many improprieties were attributed to Brandeis but nothing concrete could be proved; however, if so many people believed Brandeis to be untrustworthy and dishonest, there must be some truth to the charges; finally, even if Brandeis were totally honest, no man who was so mistrusted should be a member of a court that must be above reproach. As Lowell noted, Brandeis's "general reputation, as you know, in the better part of the Suffolk [Boston] bar is not what that of a judge should be."

Those backing the nominee also prepared their case. Publicly Brandeis refused to say anything. When a *New York Sun* reporter asked if he had heard about certain charges against him, Brandeis replied: "No I have not. I have nothing to say about anything, and that goes for all time and to all newspapers, including both the *Sun* and the moon." Privately, however, Brandeis played a central role in directing his defense. He fired off dozens of letters to Edward F. McClennen, a junior partner in his firm, who moved to Washington during the hearings to provide rebuttal evidence against the opposition charges. In these missives Brandeis responded carefully and minutely to every question raised about the propriety of his actions as a lawyer. They form an *apologia pro vita*, the nearest thing we have to a Brandeisian autobiography.

Aside from the aspersions cast upon his character and career, Brandeis found the episode extremely trying. He acceded to Attorney General Gregory's advice not to appear personally before the subcommittee and thus give the hearings an atmosphere of a trial, with himself as the defendant. Instead he relied on his associates and friends, and frequently they acted, wisely or not, in a more cautious and circumspect manner than Brandeis preferred. He wanted to defend his reputation and integrity; they wanted to establish his judicial character, which required a deliberate downplaying of the combatant role. He chafed in Boston but studiously attempted to maintain a casual demeanor. To his brother Brandeis wrote: "The Justiceship *ist ein bischen langweilig* [is a little tedious], but I am leaving the fight to others and we are getting a pretty nice issue built up. . . . Now my feeling is rather 'Go it husband, Go it bear' with myself as 'interested spectator.'"

The "interested spectator" nonetheless carefully combed his files for relevant documents, sent his supporters lists of people who could testify as to his ability and character, and kept different allies from inadvertently interfering with each other's work. More than most he realized the symbolic as well as the substantive issues involved. That "the fight has come up," he confided, "shows clearly that my instinct that I could not afford to decline was correct. It would have been, in effect, deserting the progressive forces."

The arena of the fight was the ornate Senate Judiciary Committee room in the Capitol, where the five-man subcommittee opened its hearings on February 9. Chairing the group was William E. Chilton, an intensely partisan Democrat from West Virginia not known for judicial or intellectual acuity. An equally undistinguished member was Duncan Fletcher of Florida, a man interested primarily in the price of farm products. The third Democrat was Thomas J. Walsh of Montana, at fifty-six the youngest member of the subcommittee; it was Walsh who eventually assumed the leading role in the hearings, pressing witnesses to be precise and calling for facts rather than rumors. On the Republican side sat the aging Clarence Clark of Wyoming, a Senate veteran of twenty-one years who would soon be replaced by another colorless Republican stalwart, John D. Weeks of California. The fifth member was also a Republican, but Albert Baird Cummins of Iowa was nationally known as a progressive, and some hoped that he would vote conscience rather than party. Cummins had his eye on the presidency, however, and did not care to take a stand that might offend potential conservative supporters.

The first few days of hearings were sheer chaos, with charges and rebuttals flying around the room. Clifford Thorne, chairman of the Iowa Board of Railroad Commissioners and reputed to be a reformer, led off the attack, charging Brandeis with being "guilty of infidelity, breach of faith, and unprofessional conduct in connection with one of the great cases of this generation." In the *Five Percent* case of 1913 Thorne had represented midwestern shippers opposed to the railroads' requested rate increases. Brandeis had been invited by the Interstate Commerce Commission to serve as "counsel to the situation," that is, to advise the ICC on matters relating to the fairness of rates to both shippers and roads. Thorne conceded that Brandeis had not been hired by the shippers, but he declared that the Boston attorney had betrayed the public interest by supporting a larger rate of return than did Thorne's clients. Amazingly this initial testimony questioning Brandeis's fitness centered on the nominee's alleged tenderness toward business, and Brandeis's opponents were hardly enthralled by this turn of events. "If what Thorne had to say against Brandeis is all there is," wrote William Taft, "I should not regard it as a serious matter." Taft waited hopefully for more damning evidence.

Over the next few days serious charges were indeed presented to the committee by men who had tilted with Brandeis in either business or reform matters; in nearly every case they had been on the losing side and now complained of Brandeis's tactics and activities. Finally, on February 16 the opposition moved to coordinate its campaign by bringing in Austen George Fox, a sixty-six-year-old Wall Street lawyer well connected with America's business community. As Senator Fletcher explained, Fox had come to Washington "at the request of and under employment by certain of those who oppose the confirmation of Mr. Brandeis. He suggests that he could arrange the testimony in an orderly way and see to the presentation of the facts supporting the opposition to the confirmation."

That same day Fletcher announced that George W. Anderson, a United States attorney in Boston, had been added to the subcommittee's staff to see "that the other side is presented, to the end that the truth may be determined." Anderson had been an ally of Brandeis in several civic campaigns, and although they had parted company on some issues, notably the sliding scale, the two had remained friends. His own knowledge of Brandeis's activities, backed up by Ned McClennen's copious memoranda, would now ensure an adequate rebuttal to all attacks; hostile witnesses would not be able to denounce Brandeis without substantiating their charges. Yet with the appointment of Fox and Anderson, the subcommittee hearings became just what Gregory had feared, a trial, with the defendant absent from the dock.

The opposition could not prove that Brandeis had done anything illegal; all Fox could establish was that Brandeis had practiced law in an unusual manner. Frequently Fox's witnesses wound up buttressing the case for Brandeis. For example, Fox called New York lawyer Waddill Catchings to the stand in an effort to show that Brandeis, while acting for one side in the 1907 proxy fight for control of the Illinois Central Railroad, had secretly served as an attorney for the Harriman railroad interests. Catchings at the time had been associated with Sullivan & Cromwell and had gone to Boston to secure Brandeis's services. As it turned out, this work was unrelated to Illinois Central matters and took place afterward. Moreover, Catchings said, he had been warned that the Boston firm would not accept the business "unless Mr. Brandeis was convinced of the justness of our position. . . . I accordingly had to lay the situation before Mr. Brandeis, and I may say that the hardest interview I had during the whole campaign was with Mr. Brandeis in convincing him of the justness of our cause, so to speak."

Several other witnesses called by Fox also slipped out of his hands, and their testimony merely confirmed the unorthodoxy of Brandeis's legal career rather than any wrongdoing. Ironically the problem frequently appeared to be that Brandeis had been called in not as an advocate but as "counsel to the situation." In trying to be fair to both sides, in trying to be *judicious*, he had left some of the participants unsure as to just where he stood. Brandeis's impartiality thus became a reason for barring him from judicial office!

The hundreds of pages of testimony taken in the hearings revealed that Brandeis as a lawyer did not conform to the model deemed acceptable by Boston's State Street establishment and their allies in New York's financial district. Among Boston lawyers, Moorefield Storey declared, Brandeis's reputation was "that of a man who is an able lawyer, very energetic, ruthless in his attainment of his objectives, not scrupulous in the methods he adopts, and not to be trusted." Yet Storey, like the others who echoed this opinion, could not pinpoint a single instance of unethical behavior.

What angered the Brahmins was that Brandeis, a graduate of Harvard Law School and a man who had given every indication of becoming a fine — and trusted — corporate lawyer, had broken away to become a reformer, and the targets of his reforms had frequently been Boston's own social and economic elite. Moreover, the puritanical Brandeis, who had to be convinced of the rightness of a client's case, did not mix easily with this elite. As one witness explained: "I think if Mr. Brandeis had been a different sort of man, not so aloof, not so isolated, with more of the camaraderie of the bar, gave his confidence to more men, and took their confidence . . . you would not hear the things you have heard in regard to him. But Mr. Brandeis is aloof."

The increasing tempo of the attack on Brandeis showed how isolated he was from proper society. At William Howard Taft's behest six other former presidents of the American Bar Association joined him in a letter to the subcommittee declaring that "in their opinion taking into view the reputation, character and professional career of Mr. Louis D. Brandeis, he is not a fit person to be a member of the Supreme Court of the United States." In Boston fifty-five prominent citizens, headed by Harvard's A. Lawrence Lowell, signed a petition opposing confirmation. "We do not believe," they wrote, "that Mr. Brandeis has the judicial temperament and capacity which should be required in a judge of the Supreme Court. His reputation as a lawyer is such that he has not the confidence of the people."

Proper Boston resented this outsider, this Jew, who adhered more closely to the old Massachusetts principles than they did, who was too successful (i.e., not "gentlemanly") in his profession, and who had defeated them time after time. J. Butler Studley, a lawyer in Brandeis's office, drew up a chart showing how all fifty-five were interconnected through private clubs, corporate directorships, Back Bay residences, and intermarriage. As Walter Lippmann (himself a Harvard graduate) editorialized in the *New Republic,* Brandeis had been found guilty of being "a rebellious and troublesome member of the most homogeneous, self-centered, and self-complacent community in the United States. . . . He was untrustworthy because he was troublesome. He was disloyal, if at all, to a group." Charles Francis Adams had once written: "I have tried Boston socially on all sides. I have summered and wintered it, tried it drunk and tried it sober, and drunk or sober there is nothing in it save Boston. . . . It is, so to speak, stationary — a world, a Boston world unto itself, and like all things stationary, it tends to stagnate." In this stagnant pool, as it were, Brandeis had made waves.

Finally, on March 15 the subcommittee hearings dragged to a close. Fox still wanted to parade several dozen more character witnesses before the senators, but even the Republicans had had enough. As the five legislators retired to deliberate, Brandeis's opponents stepped up their campaign, and their actions had more of the appearance of professional misconduct than anything they had alleged against Brandeis. For example, Austen Fox and his colleague, Kenneth Spence, prepared an official-looking document that on first glance appeared to be the report of the subcommittee. In it they rehashed all the allegations presented in the hearings and came to the conclusion that Brandeis was unfit to hold public office. The attack was mailed broadside to nearly every lawyer in the country, and many of them protested the nature of the piece.

On April 3 the subcommittee announced its decision. By a three-to-two vote along party lines, it approved the Brandeis nomination. Senators Chilton and Fletcher wrote the majority report; Senator Walsh concurred in a separate and more emphatic statement; both Cummins and Weeks sent in lengthy and strongly worded condemnations of the nominee. The scene now shifted to the full Senate Judiciary Committee, where the outcome still remained very much in doubt.

Responsibility for shepherding the nomination through the committee passed from Chilton to Charles A. Culberson of Texas, an eighteen-year veteran of the Senate now suffering from paralysis agitans. Culberson could no longer deliver speeches; he could hardly utter two sentences before his affliction caused him to stutter badly. But his mental faculties were still acute, and he recognized that while the eight Republican members would oppose the nomination, not all ten Democrats were fully sympathetic. Chilton, Fletcher, and Walsh could be counted upon; Culberson would support Brandeis out of deference to the president's wishes; and young Henry Ashhurst of Arizona favored the appointment.

Of the remaining five Democrats each had some reason to vote in the negative. Lee Overman of North Carolina had once been a railroad president, and Brandeis had been a foe of railroad rate increases. James O'Gorman of New York was at odds with Wilson and might vote no just to spite the president. Jim Reed of Missouri had his eye on the 1920 Democratic presidential nomination and wanted to test the political winds before committing himself. John Knight Shields of Tennessee and Hoke Smith of Georgia were both uncommitted and unpredictable.

Because of the uncertainty of the vote and the approaching party conventions (which kept several senators out of Washington), Culberson did not try to rush matters. Throughout April the matter hung in limbo in committee while Brandeis's foes continued to unload barrage after barrage of evidence regarding his unfitness. In turn, the nominee's advocates issued rebuttal statements and at times even went on the offensive regarding the intentions and scruples of Brandeis's detractors. At the end of April, three months after Wilson had sent in the nomination, the vacancy on the Court remained unfilled, with no sign that either the Judiciary Committee or the Senate would act soon. Then the dam broke as Wilson, Brandeis, and their allies moved from apathy to action, from defense to attack.

In Cambridge Felix Frankfurter and Roscoe Pound rounded up seven of the nine Harvard Law School professors to sign a strongly worded letter testifying to Brandeis's legal ability and integrity. A still more impressive message came from the venerated Charles W. Eliot, president emeritus of Harvard. "I have known Mr. Brandeis for forty years, and believe that I understand his capacities and his character," Eliot wrote. As a student Brandeis "possessed by nature a keen intelligence, quick and generous sympathies, a remarkable capacity for labor, and a character in which gentleness, courage and joy in combat were intimately blended. His professional career has exhibited all these qualities, and with them much practical altruism and public spirit." Eliot conceded that on some matters he and Brandeis had disagreed, but these differences had never led him to question Brandeis's ability or integrity. Brandeis's rejection, Eliot concluded, "would be a grave misfortune for the whole legal profession, the court, all American business and the country."

An even more important letter came to Culberson from the White House. Woodrow Wilson finally realized that confirmation, which he had confidently expected, now stood in jeopardy. Culberson had told the president that many Democrats would support Brandeis if they believed Wilson really wanted him confirmed, but they might abstain or even vote against the candidate if it were not a party matter. Wilson had to make clear to the senators and to the American people that he did indeed support Louis Brandeis. On May 5 Wilson wrote to Culberson fulsomely praising the nominee. He had tested Brandeis, the president declared, "by seeking his advice upon some of the most difficult and perplexing public questions." In every instance Brandeis had provided "counsel singularly enlightening, singularly clear-sighted and judicial, and above all, full of moral stimulation." The man he had named to the nation's highest court was "a friend of all just men and a lover of the right." In tone and substance the president made it clear that he wanted the nomination approved.

Wilson now sent his Secretary of the Navy Josephus Daniels to talk to Hoke Smith of Georgia about Brandeis. And on Sunday evening, May 14, both Smith and Jim Reed dropped in for a drink at the Washington apartment of journalist Norman Hapgood to discover that Louis Brandeis was there. Reed had intended to stay for just a moment and in fact had left Mrs. Reed waiting in the car. But he lost track of time as he and Brandeis sat and spoke for more than an hour. By the time he left, Reed had sized up all the political factors and was impressed by the nominee; he would vote for Brandeis. A similar conversion took place when Brandeis turned to Hoke Smith after Reed left; two more Democrats had fallen into line.

The following Thursday an unforeseen event took place 3000 miles across the Atlantic. A British court-martial passed a sentence of death on Jeremiah Lynch, a naturalized American citizen and New York resident who had returned to his native land to participate in the Irish struggle for independence. Lynch's sentence was to be carried out at midnight, and Senator O'Gorman, the pride of New York's Irish community, suddenly forgot all his old grievances against Woodrow Wilson and sought his help in preventing Lynch's execution. The next day's papers told the story of how Wilson, at O'Gorman's request, had cabled the American ambassador in London directing him to make every possible effort to save Lynch and as a result the death sentence was commuted to ten years in prison. O'Gorman, now a hero in New York, recognized his political debt to Wilson; one more vote for Brandeis's confirmation.

Two days later a tired president sat on a special train carrying him from Washington to Charlotte, North Carolina. Wilson had reluctantly agreed to attend the annual celebration of the Mecklenburg Declaration of 1775 as a favor to Secretary of the Navy Josephus Daniels and the state's two senators. As the train approached Salisbury, Lee Overman's hometown, the senator pleaded through Daniels for the president to stop for a brief appearance. Wilson at first declined, but the politically astute Daniels immediately saw the importance of such a gesture. Wilson then agreed, and as Overman proudly introduced the president of the United States to his friends and neighbors, Wilson launched into an impromptu talk praising Overman and all those "forward-looking men" who supported his programs and his appointments. As the train rolled back to Washington that evening, Josephus Daniels happily informed Wilson that Overman would vote for confirmation.

The last of the uncommitted Democrats was John Knight Shields of Tennessee. Wilson's son-in-law, Secretary of the Treasury William Gibbs McAdoo, had grown up in that state, and he utilized all his old contacts to get the message through to Shields that Tennesseans supported the president's nomination. Wilson himself went out of his way to consult Shields on several minor matters. Since Tennessee's other senator, Luke Lea, had been defeated in the Democratic primary, Shields now realized he would be the state's senior senator, and his ability to influence patronage at home would depend upon maintaining good relations with the White House.

The troops had rallied, and Culberson scheduled the vote on the appointment for Wednesday morning, May 24. By a straight party vote of ten to eight, the full Judiciary Committee recommended that Brandeis be confirmed. Victory was now certain. Because of the party lineups in both the Judiciary Committee and the subcommittee, Democrats in the full Senate would support the president's man as a matter of party discipline.

The end came a few minutes before five in the afternoon on June 1, 1916. With the galleries cleared the Senate went into executive session. At half-past five the doors opened, and Vice-President Thomas Marshall announced that Louis D. Brandeis had been confirmed as associate justice of the United States Supreme Court by a vote of 47 to 22. Of the Democrats only Francis Newlands of Nevada had voted no. Among the Republicans three insurgent progressives, LaFollette of Wisconsin, George Norris of Nebraska, and Miles Poindexter of Washington, voted for Brandeis, and two others, Clapp of Minnesota and Gronna of North Dakota, were absent but paired on the "aye" side.

While the Senate was still in executive session, Brandeis had left his office and taken the late afternoon train to his summer home in Dedham. As he opened the door, his wife greeted him with "Good evening, Mr. Justice Brandeis." The long fight was over. Progressives across the nation rejoiced in the victory, but Brandeis himself still had mixed emotions about the entire affair. "There is so much that I should like to do," he told Walter Douglas, his old law school roommate, "that can be done only by one out of office, that going even upon the Supreme Court Bench involves important sacrifices." Yet when Amos Pinchot wrote how much he and other progressives would miss Brandeis by their side in the battles ahead, the new justice replied that he had been bound to accept the nomination when offered, although he had realized fully what acceptance involved.

The efforts of those who sought to defeat confirmation had resolved his doubts. "The struggle certainly was worthwhile. It has defined the issues. It has been a great education to a large number of people; perhaps even to judges. And I trust it may prove possible for me to render service of real value on the Bench."

At the age of sixty, one of America's leading reformers prepared to start a new career, and that June evening in Dedham was ripe with anticipation as well as triumph. As he read through the pile of telegrams that flooded in, one in particular caught his eye. It read "WELCOME" and was signed Oliver Wendell Holmes.

VII

Transition

WHEN A MAN dons the silk robe, Judge Jerome Frank once commented, he does not slough off habits and beliefs accumulated over a lifetime. Louis Brandeis's appointment to the United States Supreme Court did not create a schism in his life but merely marked the transfer of his activities from one arena to another. The progressive philosophy for which he had fought in municipal, state, and national reform battles would now be defended in the hallowed halls of the nation's highest court, with less heat and acrimony, perhaps, but with fully developed intellectual resources and an eloquence that at times surprised even his most ardent admirers.

The transition from Citizen Brandeis to Mr. Justice Brandeis was not without its moments of discomfort, but as the years passed he would wear the role of jurist and elder statesman so naturally that many forgot he had once been characterized as a radical and an anarchist. His lean frame and constant exercise had always made him appear younger than his years, and now as he aged, he did so gracefully, the shock of white hair over craggy features giving him an almost patriarchal aura. "Isaiah," Franklin Roosevelt would call him, a name that caught the veneration accorded him by two generations of reformers.

Because of the heavy case load confronting the Court, a burden magnified by the five-month vacancy, both Chief Justice Edward White and Attorney General Thomas W. Greg-

ory urged Brandeis to be sworn in immediately after confirmation. On the last day of the term, June 5, 1916, Louis
Dembitz Brandeis took the oath of associate justice, and for
one of the few times in his life he appeared nervous. But by
the time the Court convened the following October, Brandeis
had prepared himself for his new role. He had resigned from
nearly all his reform associations with the exception of Zionism, closed out his business connection with his Boston law
firm, put his financial affairs in order, and found a modest
apartment in Washington's Stoneleigh Court. One of his
more important decisions was to do away with a regular
secretary; instead, each year he took on as an assistant a
bright young graduate of the Harvard Law School whom
Felix Frankfurter selected for him. Among those who served
this apprenticeship were Dean Acheson, James Landis, Paul
Freund, David Riesman, Willard Hurst, and Adrien Fisher.

The man who as a youngster so loved the law had, throughout his life, considered the bench as the place where the logic
of the law could reach its fullest and most noble expression.
He had criticized judges for failing to deal with a living law;
he complained that by ignoring the realities of life, judges
had demeaned their high office in the public's eyes. Brandeis
determined that nothing he would say or do, either in his
official capacity or off the bench, would in any way reflect
adversely on the Supreme Court. He severed formal relations
with reform groups, refused to accept invitations for public
appearances or give interviews, and adopted a public posture
that many came to consider the very model of judicial recti-
tude. Through twenty-three years on the bench there is not a
single letter regarding the workings of the Court or how the
justices reached their decisions. He even refused to accept
honorary degrees, to avoid any impression that his opinions
on the Court were somehow being rewarded.

Yet Brandeis was also a realist, and for all his adult life he
had been an activist, a fighter for causes in which he believed.
One could not simply reverse the pattern of decades nor
ignore the relations developed in shared battles. The presi-

dent had valued his advice; it would not be fair to him or to the country during the crisis of war to withhold his counsel. Nor could Brandeis abandon the Zionist movement or the fight for democracy in American Jewish life. His first years on the Supreme Court thus required him to feel his way carefully as he made the transition from advocate to arbitrator, from activist to adviser. He made several mistakes, but never the same one twice, and within a relatively short time he worked out the manner in which he would reconcile these antipodal demands. Most of the time he did so with grace and precision, but on occasion he violated his own canons of conduct.

In some ways the transition from the people's attorney to Mr. Justice proved less difficult than anticipated. Brandeis after all knew the law, both in principle and in practice. He had been a superb technician as an attorney, and he proved to be perhaps the finest legal craftsman ever to sit on the high court. The techniques he had developed in preparing cases such as *Muller* v. *Oregon* for argument transferred easily to preparing opinions, and he now had a new and greater forum than ever before from which he could advocate the principles of a living law. As a lawyer he had attempted to educate bench and bar to the need of law conforming to reality; that campaign never ceased. Nearly all his law clerks recalled how, after they had searched out every conceivable facet of the law on a specific case, the justice would say: "Now I think the opinion is persuasive, but what can we do to make it more instructive?"

Despite earlier misgivings about joining the Court, by the fall of 1916 he looked foward with eagerness to his first term. "There is much to be done which promises to be very interesting," he wrote Alfred, "and I have the utmost confidence." Few other appointees ever brought such an impressive set of credentials to the bench as did Brandeis. Not only did he know the law in abstract, but his knowledge extended into the realms of everyday affairs. Economics, statistics, psychology, politics, labor relations, rate regulation — his experience encompassed them all. While he knew that he would be fighting a conservative majority among his brethren, he certainly did not feel overawed at the prospect; privately he probably welcomed the battle. To have joined eight like-minded men would have held no appeal for a latter-day knight-errant.

Throughout his twenty-three years on the bench, most of his more than five hundred opinions were written for the majority; in the wide spectrum of cases that reached the Court, Brandeis usually found it possible either to join with his colleagues or to win them over to his point of view. But there is no doubt that his great contribution to American constitutional development came in dissent, in those cases where he spoke for a living law, for a justice attuned to modern American society. Some of these cases involved personal liberty and welfare, others the interrelated powers and limits of governments within a federal system. In all of them his motto might well have been two sentences he wrote in the *Oklahoma Ice* case: "In the exercise of [our] high power, we must be ever on guard, lest we erect our prejudices into legal principles. If we would guide by the light of reason, we must let our minds be bold."

The pattern of the Brandeisian method, so familiar to those who had followed his earlier reform activities, quickly asserted itself on the bench. He utilized every opportunity to instruct his brethren and the public on why the tribunal had decided in a certain manner, or why he believed it had been wrong in doing so. His very first dissent in *New York Central* v. *Winfield* (1917), a case in which the majority held that a federal employers' liability act had preempted the field from the states, set the pattern. "The importance of the question involved" induced him "to state the reasons" for his dissent, which he then bolstered with extensive references to past decisions as well as a dissertation on the nature, origin, and purpose of the Federal Employers Liability Act, including "world experience in dealing with industrial accidents."

His second dissent protested the Court's overturning of a state statute regulating private employment agencies without even inquiring into the conditions that had led to its enactment (*Adams* v. *Tanner*). "The judgment," he lectured his brethren, "should be based upon a consideration of relevant facts, actual or possible — *ex factor jus oritur*. The ancient rule must prevail in order that we have a system of living law. . . . What was the evil which the people of Washington sought to correct? Why was the particular remedy embodied in the statute adopted? And, incidentally, what has been the experience, if any, of other states or countries in this connection?" He then went on to justify the law, not in narrow legal terms but as a legitimate response to a real social problem, which he also described in great detail. Justice John H. Clarke, who together with Oliver Wendell Holmes joined in the dissent, scribbled on the draft copy "only the Lord can so harden their heads as well as their hearts as to prevent their confessing their sin of ignorance." Just as he had shown lawyers how to use economic and sociological data in the *Muller* brief, now he would try to impress upon his colleagues the necessity of understanding and evaluating the real world while handing down legal dicta from their sanctuary.

Because so much of the Court's business at the time involved economic questions, Brandeis was particularly well qualified to inject more life into the law; few people of his generation understood so well the inner workings of the economic system. His old love of facts and then more facts, one of the qualities that had made him a brilliant lawyer, now contributed to his greatness as a judge. One of the best examples of Brandeis utilizing his economic understanding and background can be found in his concurring opinion in *Southwestern Bell Telephone Company* v. *Public Service Commission of Missouri*, a statement characterized by one scholar as the ablest critique ever made on the economics of utility valuation.

When states had first passed legislation regulating public utilities, the courts, exercising judicial restraint, had declined to interfere with the administrative agencies. By 1898, however, with conservatives in full control of the judicial branch, judges began injecting their own biases into the issue; in *Smyth*

v. *Ames* the Supreme Court arrogated unto judicial review the whole question of what constituted fair and reasonable rates. The Court declared that under the aegis of the Fourteenth Amendment public utility companies would be deprived of property without due process unless they received a fair return on their property. While few quarreled with that premise, the Court had gone on to establish a formula based on current valuation of the property as the basis for a fair rate. The problem lay in the fact that current valuation was exceedingly difficult to determine, and if a company felt that a regulatory commission had not been generous enough, it could appeal to the courts. A determined corporation could emasculate the state or local regulatory agency by claiming deprivation of property without due process. Judges frequently were more sympathetic to the corporate viewpoint than regulatory commissions, but they did not have the expertise necessary to evaluate the complicated data involved in rate setting.

In 1922 the Supreme Court reversed the Missouri Supreme Court, which had upheld a Public Service Commission order reducing telephone rates. Mr. Justice McReynolds in delivering the opinion charged that the Commission's directed rates did not provide a fair return upon invested capital, and that it had been especially negligent in its valuation of the company's property according to the *Smyth* v. *Ames* formula. Brandeis, while concurring in the decision, announced that "I differ fundamentally from my brethren concerning the rule to be applied," and then went on to attack the entire basis of present value as a criterion for return.

By carefully tracing economic trends, Brandeis demonstrated how any attempt to determine current value could end only in chaos. Prices fluctuated from year to year, even from week to week. Since the worth of a utility depended to a large extent on its earnings, and its earnings upon rates, and its rates upon valuation, the whole enterprise became one vicious circle. Relentlessly elaborating upon every defect in the system, Brandeis tried to show that the old rule, while it may have had some legal justification, did not make any economic sense.

Characteristically, Brandeis did not stop with an attack on a faulty system but went on to propose a constructive alternative in its place. Drawing upon his experience with the Public Franchise League and the Interstate Commerce Commission, he suggested the adoption of the "prudent investment principle," which would assure a return commensurate with that of private capital prudently invested. While this method had its own complexities, it nonetheless had the benefit of a more easily ascertainable rate, one that broke down the cycle of value-return-rate-value. Moreover, once methods and standards had been arrived at, the courts could withdraw from involvement in the regulatory procedures and leave the administrative agencies as the prime instruments of control.

Brandeis's support of the prudent investment principle had evolved from his earlier work in Massachusetts and with the ICC and clearly demonstrated how he continued to uphold the progressive tradition after he left the ranks of active reformers to join the bench. He had always believed that private capital invested in public utilities deserved a fair return, as he had argued in the sliding scale proposal. Because of the special status of businesses concerned with the public interest, however, great care had to be taken that the return remained fair and not exorbitant. He had crusaded for years to get state agencies and the ICC to adopt modern and uniform principles of accounting, in order to agree on fair and reasonable formulas that could be easily understood and ascertained and that would do justice to both investors and the public. Few areas of concern were so complicated as rate setting, and few better illustrated the progressive faith in economic rationalization and the public utilization of expertise.

Few of Brandeis's colleagues on the Court accepted the prudent investment principle as a sound basis for rate making or even his legal arguments that the prime responsibility for regulation lay with the administrative agencies. Probably only

Pierce Butler, a former railroad attorney, understood some of Brandeis's arguments, but as an archconservative he viewed the Court as a bastion against the semisocialistic regulatory commissions. The rest of the Court remained ignorant about the economics of the matter, a problem that Brandeis would address time and time again until he had finally educated enough people to remove rate making from judicial hands.

If the assumption of judicial duties proved relatively easy, the adjustment to his new role off the Court turned out to be far more difficult. His deep personal commitment to Woodrow Wilson, to democracy in Jewish life, and to Zionism did not allow him to detach himself from active participation.

The first step in this extrajudicial thicket showed him how difficult a role he would have to play now that he had left the freedom of private life. Although he had resigned from nearly all reform activities, he still hoped he might have active, if less visible, tasks in those most dear to his heart. This situation proved possible in the case of savings bank life insurance, where he channeled his advice through his former secretary, Alice Harriet Grady, who later became deputy commissioner for the program. When he interested himself in legal education at the Harvard Law School and in the development of the University of Louisville, he also found surrogates to act for him. But in the fight for the American Jewish Congress and in Zionism, he stood too identified in the public mind to step aside. It might have been better had he attempted to do so, but despite his awareness of the political dangers, he refused to abandon his followers in the midst of the fight.

The battle for the Jewish congress had all but been won by the time the Senate confirmed Brandeis's nomination, but he and his colleagues still hoped to reach an understanding with the American Jewish Committee. In mid-June the Committee asked for a meeting of representatives of the major Jewish organizations together with the congress leaders to see if some grounds for unity still existed. It was, as Louis Marshall, Brandeis, and the others all recognized, a signal from the

Committee that it was conceding defeat and now wanted to salvage, with some dignity, a place in the new order. The congress organizers agreed with Brandeis that instead of excluding the *yahudim,* some way should be found to bring them back into the community. They still controlled much wealth and enjoyed great prestige; to freeze them out would only hurt the Jewish cause.

The Committee sensed this, and it adopted a strategy based on the desire of its opponents to make peace and also on the fact that Brandeis, whether he recognized it or not, was now circumscribed in his freedom to maneuver. At the Hotel Astor meeting July 16 they deliberately insulted him, made impossible demands, and then charged the downtown Jews with being autocratic in their refusal to compromise. Two days later the *New York Times,* obviously speaking for the Committee, published a lengthy editorial entitled "Out of Place," which took Brandeis to task for violating tbe custom "faithfully honored by observance, for the Justices of the Supreme Court of the United States, upon taking office, to withdraw from many activities of a political or social nature, in which as private citizens they were free to engage, in order . . . to avoid all controversies which might seem in any degree to affect their judicial impartiality of mind." Ignoring the fact that the Committee leaders had precipitated the attack, the *Times* piously noted that it was unseemly for a Supreme Court justice to have been involved in such a verbal donnybrook.

Brandeis recognized that he had been trapped and also saw that he could not escape. To try to set the record straight would only engender further controversy, and he feared tarnishing his newly acquired judicial stature even before his first full term on the bench. On July 21, without consulting any of his associates, he resigned all his offices in the American Jewish Congress, the Joint Distribution Committee, the American Jewish Relief Committee, and the Provisional Executive Committee. He acknowledged that the Hotel Astor incident, even though deliberately provoked, had shown that he could no longer act as if he were a private citizen. "There is at least this compensation," he wrote, "my enforced withdrawal did not come until after the triumph of the Congress movement has been made possible." Despite impassioned pleas from his followers, Brandeis, having made his decision, refused to budge. The situation had been much too awkward and he would not risk a similar episode in the future. As he told Jacob deHaas, although non-Jews did not seem to object to his retaining leadership in the Zionist movement, many Jews did, and this created obstacles that would inevitably prove embarrassing.

But if Brandeis could turn a deaf ear to the congress organizers, he could not do so to a request from the president of the United States, one that, although having precedents, still endangered his status on the Court. Wilson asked him to lead a commission to settle the border dispute with Mexico, a situation that threatened to plunge both countries into an unwanted war. Here, if Brandeis so chose, he could find justification for acceptance, for ever since Chief Justice John Jay had, at President Washington's request, negotiated a treaty with England in 1794, presidents had from time to time availed themselves of the services of Supreme Court justices in nonjudicial missions.

Brandeis trod carefully this time. He interrupted his own vacation on Cape Cod to travel to Lake Placid, where Chief Justice White was summering. The older jurist, who had already given Brandeis sound advice on how to arrange his financial matters, prevailed on his new colleague to decline Wilson's request. The large backlog of judicial work could be the excuse to the president; the real reason, however, lay in White's belief, in which Brandeis concurred, that the Court should remain aloof from the affairs of the legislative and executive branches, affairs that might conceivably come under judicial scrutiny in the future.

Several times during the next three years the president would be urged to appoint Brandeis to an important administrative position. "I need Brandeis everywhere," Wilson once told Rabbi Stephen Wise. Robert Wooley, a reformer, related a conversation in which Wilson said: "When a seemingly impossible war emergency task looms, I am urged to draft Brandeis to tackle it. At least twice I have put it up to him. Very properly he replied that he would take it up with the Chief Justice. In each instance Chief Justice White held that a member of the Supreme Court should confine his endeavors to the work of the Court. I readily agreed. Whereupon Brandeis would offer to resign, which was characteristic of him. My reply was: 'Not on your life. On that Bench you are more important to the Country than you could possibly be elsewhere. It was too difficult to get you there to take a chance on losing you through a temporary arrangement.'"

Nevertheless, Wilson frequently turned to Brandeis for advice. Both men had an exquisite sense of the proprieties of the situation, yet each felt that the needs of the country justified their continued collaboration. For the most part they communicated through intermediaries, usually Secretary of the Navy Josephus Daniels. Brandeis occasionally discovered someone whom he felt could be of real service to the war program and undertook discreetly to bring him to the attention of administration officials. A series of conferences Brandeis arranged with Secretary of the Army Newton D. Baker and Treasury Secretary William Gibbs McAdoo led to the appointment of Herbert Hoover as food administrator. A number of men in the war government took to visiting Brandeis on a more or less regular basis, seeking out his analyses of difficult problems, either for their own benefit or for transmission to the president.

Some matters, however, were too delicate to be left to messengers, and here Wilson showed himself as sensitive to protocol as the man he had appointed to the high court. Late in 1917 the entire war effort seemed on the verge of collapse due to the failure to coordinate domestic manufacturing and distribution. The New Freedom's original hostility to big government proved not only irrelevant but destructive in wartime. A country at war could not afford an unregulated economy; it needed coordination, control, and direction. Endless bottlenecks and delays in the rail network kept raw materials from factories and prevented finished goods from reaching eastern ports for transshipment to the European front. As the industrial war machine bogged down, the administration came under increasing pressure to appoint wartime czars to supervise key components of the economy. Wilson, aware of the need to increase production and improve distribution, yet still fearful of centralized authority, turned as he often did to Brandeis.

The most pressing problem involved coordination of the railroads, and several government officials urged Wilson to name William Gibbs McAdoo director general. Wilson agreed that McAdoo was undoubtedly the ablest person in the cabinet; yet he already held the important and powerful post of treasury secretary, and beyond that he was the president's son-in-law. Joseph Tumulty, the presidential secretary, sent a message that Wilson wanted advice about the appointment; Brandeis, however, refused to go to the White House to argue in McAdoo's behalf.

Later in the day Mrs. Brandeis answered a knock at her front door to discover the president of the United States standing there together with two Secret Service men. When the justice came out, Wilson commented: "I could not request you to come to me, and I have therefore come to you to ask your advice." The two men retired to the study, where amidst law books and papers strewn about the room, they discussed the problem of coordinating the nation's railroads and whether McAdoo should be given the job. Although Brandeis preferred that McAdoo relinquish the Treasury rather than take on both jobs, the president, now reassured, chose to keep McAdoo on both jobs, where, in fact, he did quite well.

The following month, January 1918, Wilson again turned to Brandeis for advice on a similar problem. To centralize power in manufacturing in effect meant abandoning the New Freedom; not to do so would endanger the Allied war program. This time the medium of exchange was Colonel Edward

M. House, and in a lengthy letter Brandeis confirmed the increasing need for a greater centralized authority.

This advice was not contrary to all that Brandeis had previously stood for; he remained true to his first principles. He was not so close-minded to pretend, as did some of Wilson's advisers, that the country could go on undisturbed during the war. New crises demanded new approaches, but basic principles could be sustained. Brandeis urged clear lines of responsibility. Men were trying to do too much; administrators had to restrict themselves to what they could accomplish. The government already had the necessary powers but had failed to utilize them effectively. The answer lay not in granting more power, but in delineating specifically who would do what, giving that person the necessary latitude and authority, and then holding him strictly accountable for performance.

Again Wilson heeded Brandeis's counsel, and soon afterward he created the War Industries Board headed by Bernard Baruch. The quiet intercourse between president and justice profited both men; Wilson needed the reassurance that in centralizing responsibilities he was not abandoning reform, while Brandeis still yearned to be of service in the arena of active affairs.

In one area, however, Brandeis saw all the action he wanted and suffered the most stinging defeat of his career. After the Hotel Astor incident Brandeis had formally resigned from all his Jewish offices, but devotion to Zionism led him to retain the honorary chairmanship of the movement. While Stephen Wise and Julian Mack directed daily affairs, they consulted with him constantly. A steady stream of letters, telegrams, directives, memoranda, and reminders flowed out of Stoneleigh Court, and in the major policy decisions between 1916 and 1921, Brandeis remained the leader of American Zionism. In 1917 as Great Britain, unsure of American reaction, hesitated over issuing the Balfour Declaration, Brandeis convinced Wilson to endorse the English promise to reestablish a Jewish homeland in Palestine after the fighting ended.

Zionism in America, in fact, flourished during the war years. The Balfour Declaration and American approval of it helped eliminate much anti-Zionist feeling. By the Armistice in November 1918 the movement in the United States counted over 186,000 members, more than fifteen times what it had been when Brandeis took over the chairmanship of the Provisional Committee in August 1914. This growth created new problems, however, for the old system of independent societies made coordination difficult. Just as he had reorganized the Provisional Committee, now Brandeis embarked on a larger restructuring of the movement and also provided it with the most concise ideological statement of what Zionism meant in the United States. Here again Brandeis acted upon the progressive tradition, but in doing so he ran head-on into another, and at that time more powerful, tradition, that of European Zionism.

The reorganization proved relatively easy to accomplish. The majority of Zionist leaders conceded that consolidation, with leadership concentrated in a single office, was a necessary step. The final merger came in 1918, when the Provisional Committee, the Federation of American Zionists, and other units joined to form the Zionist Organization of America, based upon individual rather than club membership and organized into geographical units. Within the ZOA certain groups, such as Hadassah and Young Judea, retained their separate identities. The Poale Zion (socialist Zionists) stayed outside of the ZOA but agreed to cooperate closely. Only the Mizrachi, the religious bloc, stayed completely aloof, but it had also been the only American Zionist group that had refused to subordinate its American activities to the Provisional Committee.

With the creation of the ZOA the Brandeis leadership converted American Zionism into an effective instrument for the dissemination of Zionist ideas, the raising of funds, and the wielding of political influence. The ZOA marked the final step on the road Brandeis had first taken in his work with the

Provisional Committee; the lessons learned by the progressives in their reform activities proved equally valuable in their pursuit of Zionist goals.

At the same convention in Pittsburgh in 1918 that saw the adoption of the reorganization plan, Brandeis presented an ideological program. With the Balfour Declaration in hand, Jerusalem captured by the British army, and the war progressing well, he believed the time ripe to state just what American Zionists wanted and the means they intended to utilize in achieving those ends. The Basle Programme of 1897 had sought an international charter through which to re-create a Jewish homeland in Palestine, but it had not attempted to define the nature of that homeland. With the end of the war practical work would begin to turn Herzl's dream into a reality, and the Brandeis group had very definite ideas as to what the new Zion should be. Written primarily by Brandeis, with the aid of Horace Meyer Kallen, the six-point document convincingly demonstrated the pervasive influence of progressive reform in American Zionism. After a token nod at the principles of Jewish law "embodied in the traditions of two thousand years," the Pittsburgh platform called for political and civil equality for all the inhabitants of Palestine, irrespective of race, sex, or faith. Natural resources, including land, would be owned by the entire people, to avoid exploitation by private interests. The economy would be neither capitalist nor socialist, but "the cooperative principle should be applied in . . . agricultural, industrial, commercial and financial undertakings." To ensure an enlightened and informed citizenry, the state would provide free public education at all levels. About the only traditional point in the Pittsburgh platform called for Hebrew as the national language of the Jewish people. In all its aspects the document accurately reflected the basic concerns of a generation of progressive reformers rather than the nationalistic yearnings of the different Zionist groups. Its very Americanism had made the Brandeis leadership possible, but it also had prevented it from sharing in the emotional fervor of labor or religious Zionists. With the adoption of the Pittsburgh platform, the ultimate statement of an Americanized Zionism based upon progressive ideas, the troubles of the Brandeis regime began in earnest.

The bulk of American Zionists still clung to the much more religious or socialist-oriented ideologies of European Zionism, with their messianic fervor and political complexities. Their heads followed Brandeis, but the Zionism in their hearts was much more fervent than intellectual, more Jewish than American. For these first-generation immigrants the spokesman for true Zionism was not Louis Brandeis but Chaim Weizmann, the brilliant Russian-born chemist who now headed the English Zionist Federation and who had secured the Balfour Declaration.

Although relations between Brandeis and Weizmann had started out in friendly fashion, by the end of the war the two men were warily eyeing each other. Weizmann did not understand the Americans, and he constantly denigrated their commitment to Zionism. When the British had asked him to head a commission to Palestine in 1918 to investigate conditions there, he and his colleagues immediately had packed their bags. When he had asked Brandeis to join the commission, or at least to send an American delegation, Brandeis had refused. The State Department had reminded the jurist that the United States was not at war with Turkey, and it would be undiplomatic for Americans to participate in such a venture. Brandeis understood this; he was, after all, an American first and then a Zionist. Weizmann and his followers placed Zionism above everything else; they saw themselves as a Jewish government-in-the-making. Those who did not share their passion were, in their eyes, second-class Zionists whose commitment was shallow at best and probably unreliable. Weizmann also feared that the growing political power of Brandeis and the ZOA might challenge the hegemony of the old-line Europeans over the World Zionist Organization (WZO).

In the summer of 1919 Brandeis made his only trip to Palestine. He traveled up and down the land, impressed by the courage of the Jewish pioneers and the beauty of the land. "It is a wonderful country," he wrote to his wife, a land "endowed with all the interest which the history of man can contribute and the deepest emotions which can stir a people. The ages-long longing, the love is all explicable now." His quick mind took in much during his sixteen days in the holy land, and he now felt that he had a realistic understanding of the practical problems facing the Zionist movement. The land had to be made ready for people by very specific tasks of sanitation and construction. It thus came as a shock, when he met with Weizmann and other European Zionist leaders in London on his way home, to discover that they could think only about political issues; practical matters, they informed the American leaders, would have to wait.

For Brandeis the Europeans had their priorities reversed. He recognized that until the Peace Conference actually awarded Palestine to Great Britain, there would be political problems. He had engaged in some of those discussions when he had met with Wilson and other world leaders during his stay in Paris; all had assured Brandeis that Palestine would be given to England for the establishment of a Jewish homeland. The political charter sought by Herzl would thus be embodied in the Balfour Declaration and in the mandate; to actually turn Palestine into a Jewish homeland would now require massive immigration, and the very top priority was the practical task of preparing the land to receive the people. For the next two years Brandeis fought vainly to convince the Europeans that they had won the initial political battles and that they should get down to concrete tasks.

The Europeans in turn demanded that the Americans raise more money, not for new ventures but to support the work of the WZO and the existing Jewish colonies in Palestine. The slipshod management Brandeis and Stephen Wise saw in the London Zionist offices did not inspire confidence; in fact, the financially conservative Brandeis was horrified by the careless monetary arrangements of the WZO. When Weizmann proposed a new money-raising venture, the Keren Hayesod

(Endowment Fund), which commingled donations and monies earmarked for investment, the Americans flatly refused to have anything to do with it. Weizmann now had his issue, and he aligned himself with those Eastern European groups in the United States most disaffected by the Brandeis leadership. He journeyed to America in the spring of 1921, ostensibly to inaugurate the Endowment Fund but actually to challenge Brandeis.

It was a one-sided battle; Brandeis would not leave the Court, a fact that Weizmann exploited to show that the American leader was not truly devoted to Zionism. The complicated financial matters that so angered Brandeis made little sense to the masses; they saw Chaim Weizmann, the personification of European Jewry, calling upon them to be Jews and turn away from assimilation, while an Americanized Louis Brandeis, hidden on the Court behind his lieutenants, prattled on about fiscal responsibility. At the 1921 ZOA convention in Cleveland, the Brandeis forces lost in a vote of confidence. Declaring that they could not follow an irresponsible leadership, Brandeis and thirty-seven members of the executive committee resigned en masse. "Our place," Brandeis announced in a letter to the delegates, "will then be as humble soldiers in the ranks to hasten by our struggle and policies, which we believe will be recognized as the only ones through which our great ends may be achieved."

In the 1920s the Brandeisians formed an opposition group to work on its own for Palestine; it was not a success, but then neither was the ZOA, which Louis Lipsky, Weizmann's American lieutenant, ran into the ground. However, despite all the time and effort and money he poured into work for Palestine, Brandeis's main efforts were spent in fulfilling the obligations of the Supreme Court. Although he continued to involve himself with Zionism, politics, and other nonjudicial matters, Brandeis kept these activities unpublicized as part of his private life.

VIII

To "Guide by the Light of Reason"

BECAUSE THEY WERE so often in agreement, and seemingly as often together in dissent, the names of Holmes and Brandeis became locked together in judicial history. In truth, during the fifteen terms of the Supreme Court in which they sat together on the bench, the two men nearly always voted on the same side in important constitutional questions. Because of Holmes's reputation for wit, his real contributions to jurisprudence, and his literary felicity, he enjoyed a reputation as the senior partner of "Holmes and Brandeis dissenting," the grand old man of judicial liberalism, aided by the brilliant craftsmanship of the younger Brandeis, fighting for a living law. In fact, a well-delineated philosophy ran through Brandeis's opinions and dissents. On the Court Brandeis remained the progressive: analyzing, arguing, teaching, holding fast to eternal verities while seeking new and innovative ways to apply them to modern social problems. Throughout the 1920s Brandeis kept the reform flame alive, always tempering idealism with a strong dose of practicality.

The convoluted problem of reconciling liberty and order confronted the Supreme Court in the issue of free speech. As a result of wartime hysteria Congress as well as several state legislatures passed antisedition laws aimed at pacifists, radicals, and other critics of the war to prevent them from undermining the nation's morale or from subverting the war effort.

Several cases growing out of these laws reached the Court beginning with *Schenck* v. *United States* in 1919, in which Holmes first enunciated his doctrine of "clear and present danger," clarified shortly afterward in the *Abrams* decision. "The question in every case," Holmes wrote, "is whether the words are used in such circumstances and are of such a nature as to create a clear and present danger that they will bring about the substantive evils that Congress has a right to prevent."

Holmes's pithiness and his skeptical nature, which refused to discount the merit of any idea, overshadowed Brandeis's equally important role in building safeguards around constitutional affirmations of civil liberties. Like Holmes, Brandeis had little use for the practical value of generalizations. The Brandeisian dissents contain hardheaded appraisals of the facts in an effort to protect the individual against the state, while at the same time recognizing that under certain conditions limitations upon civil liberties, as upon economic liberties, are necessary.

The first speech case in which Brandeis, rather than Holmes, wrote the dissenting opinion was *Schaefer* v. *United States* (1920); in it he undertook the arduous task of turning Holmes's apothegm into a constitutional doctrine. "Clear and present danger" was "a rule of reason," and the responsibility of juries and of the appellate courts was to ensure that it not be misused. "Like any other rule for human conduct it can be applied correctly only by the exercise of good judgment; and to the exercise of good judgment, calmness is, in times of deep feeling and on subjects which excite passion, as essential as fearlessness and honesty."

In the *Schaefer* case, and a week later in the *Pierce* decision, Brandeis, with Holmes concurring, insisted that feelings evoked during crisis should not be allowed to distort the real meaning of clear and present danger. In *Gilbert* v. *Minnesota* (1920), for example, Holmes had joined the majority in upholding Gilbert's conviction under a state sedition law for a speech attacking American participation in the war. Mr. Justice McKenna had declared for the majority: "The Nation was at war with Germany, armies were recruiting, and the speech was discouragement of that." Brandeis not only went to pains to see whether a real danger existed, but he recognized that the wording of the state law interfered with discussion of unpopular ideas even in peacetime. He condemned a clause forbidding the teaching of opposition to war as invading the privacy and freedom of the home in an unwarranted and dangerous manner. In times of emergency the government "may conclude that suppression of divergent opinion is imperative, because the emergency does not permit reliance upon slower conquest of error by truth." But to abridge freedom of speech involved a far greater danger, that of curtailing those rights essential to citizen participation in public affairs.

Brandeis also defended unpopular opinions elsewhere. When Zechariah Chafee faced attack by reactionary alumni at Harvard Law School, Brandeis quietly supported him. "You did a man's job," he wrote to Chafee, assuring him that "the persecution will make it more productive. By such follies is liberty made to grow, for the love of it is re-awakened." Throughout the 1920s Brandeis helped to finance Felix Frankfurter's work in defending unpopular causes, especially the Sacco and Vanzetti case. Freedom of expression was not an abstract ideal but an essential of democratic society.

As the coauthor of the right of privacy, Brandeis also sustained the right to be free from public prying and governmental inquisitiveness. In the *Olmstead* case he commented that "the right to be let alone [is] the most comprehensive of rights and the right most valued by civilized men." The framers of the Constitution "undertook to secure conditions favorable to the pursuit of happiness. They recognized the significance of man's spiritual nature, of his feelings and of his intellect. They knew that only a part of the pain, pleasure and satisfactions of life are to be found in material things. They sought to protect Americans in their beliefs, their thoughts, their emotions and their sensations. They conferred, as against the

Government, the right to be let alone." In another wiretapping case Brandeis asserted that this "dirty business" had to be stopped "in order to protect the Government. To protect it from illegal conduct of its officers. To preserve the purity of its courts." Brandeis saw, as did few others at the time, the degrading effects of such activities on the individual and on a state that perpetrated them.

Strikingly, Brandeis penned some of his most eloquent opinions in defense of civil liberties. No one, not even Holmes, ever presented so forceful an appeal as did Brandeis in the *Whitney* case (1927). "Those who won our independency by revolution were not cowards. They did not fear political change. They did not exalt order at the cost of liberty. To courageous, self-reliant men, with confidence in the power of free and fearless reasoning applied through the processes of popular government, no danger flowing from speech can be deemed clear and present, unless the incidence of the evil apprehended is so imminent that it may befall before there is opportunity for full discussion. . . . It is therefore always open to Americans to challenge a law abridging free speech and assembly by showing that there was no emergency justifying it."

Brandeis did not, however, hold that all restrictions on freedom of speech were a priori unconstitutional. At all times he adhered to the Greek ideal of balance. Holmes saw the test of abuse fairly simply: one does not cry "fire" in a crowded theater. For Brandeis, who really developed the notion of clear and present danger into a constitutional doctrine, the issues were much more complex. While he began with the assumption that the burden of proof regarding the danger of certain actions or utterances lay with the state, he never denied that a state had the power to preserve its integrity and that to do so might involve — and legitimately so — the temporary restrictions of basic rights.

One of Brandeis's primary concerns before ascending the bench had been the "curse of bigness," and his judicial writings indicate that he maintained this passion after 1916. In cases involving distinctions between large and small companies, he nearly always supported the right of the legislatures to make that differentiation. In 1928 the Quaker City Cab Company challenged a Pennsylvania statute that imposed a tax on corporations engaged in intrastate transportation. Since many taxis belonged either to individuals or to partnerships, they escaped the tax, and the company claimed that this violated the Fourteenth Amendment's guarantee of equal protection. The Court, by a six-to-three vote, struck down the law. In his dissent Brandeis addressed himself to the question of whether the distinction could be reasonable, and he decided in the affirmative. "In Pennsylvania the practice of imposing heavier burdens upon corporations dates from a time when there, as elsewhere in America, the fear of growing corporate power was common. The present heavier imposition may be a survival of an early effort to discourage the resort to that form of organization. . . . But there are still intelligent, informed, just-minded and civilized persons who believe that the rapidly growing aggregation of capital through corporations constitutes an insidious menace to the liberty of the citizen."

Similarly, Brandeis's economic inclinations shine through in *Liggett* v. *Lee* (1933), in which a majority of the Court held a Florida tax on chain stores to be invalid, also on the grounds that it violated the equal protection clause. To Brandeis the statute seemed more than reasonable, and almost reflexively he sprang to its defense in a forty-page dissent. "Businesses may become as harmful to the community by excessive size, as by monopoly or the commonly recognized restraints of trade. If the State should conclude that bigness in retail merchandising as manifested in corporate chain stores menaces the public welfare, it might prohibit the excessive size or extent of that business as it prohibits excessive size or weight in motor trucks or excessive heights in the buildings of a city. . . . The true prosperity of our past," he proclaimed in echoes of 1912, "came not from big business, but through the courage, the energy, and the resourcefulness of small men. . . . Only by reopening to them the opportunities for leadership, can confidence in our future be restored and the existing misery be overcome."

Brandeis rarely allowed his priorities to become confused. He disliked bigness and championed competition, yet he also believed that in some circumstances competition had to be restricted. In 1921 he wrote one of his more powerful dissents in defense of an "open competition plan" designed to limit pure competition. A group of hardwood manufacturers had agreed to exchange information about prices, production, and sales. This plan shifted emphasis from price competition to service and quality, an arrangement six members of the Court held to be in restraint of trade. Brandeis strongly disagreed, and he declared that the "Sherman Law does not prohibit every lessening of competition; and it certainly does not command that competition be pursued blindly." Unless some sort of regulation in the industry were imposed, the ultimate result would probably be the lessening of competition through combination.

Even more important than his attentiveness to competition was his adherence to the principles of a federal system. He believed that within that system the Supreme Court had an important, but well-defined, role to play, in which it should never attempt to answer anything other than the immediate and narrowly defined question before it. His insistence on maintaining a proper balance of powers and obligations sometimes led him into seemingly strange postures. For example, Brandeis rejected the claims, literally, of a workman, a widow, and an orphan in pursuance of a more harmonious federalism.

As with most men of strong beliefs and firm principles, occasions arose where two or more tenets of his faith were in conflict. One such case illustrated how Brandeis resolved this conflict. The 1932 case involved an Oklahoma statute requiring anyone entering the ice business to obtain a certificate of public convenience and necessity. Mr. Justice Sutherland, speaking for the Court, found the law unconstitutional, attacking the statute on the grounds that it "does not protect against monopoly, but tends to foster it." Brandeis dissented, arguing that the important issue at stake was the proper balance of powers and limitations within the federal system. Brandeis may or may not have agreed with the reasoning behind the Oklahoma statute. He did recognize, however, that the state, under the police power, had the right to deal with the Depression in a new and experimental manner. "It is one of the happy incidents of the federal system that a single courageous State may, if its citizens choose, serve as a laboratory, and try novel social and economic experiments without risk to the rest of the country."

A federal system dispersed power to the states, a concept certainly not strange for the opponent of concentration of any sort. The Court, however, also shared power in that system, and Brandeis demanded that it restrict itself to very limited functions. Whether the Court agreed with the aims of the Oklahoma statute did not matter. He appealed to his brethren to allow the system to be innovative and adaptive. "This Court has the power to prevent an experiment. We may strike down the statute which embodies it on the ground that, in our opinion, the measure is arbitrary, capricious or unreasonable. We have the power to do this, because the due process clause has been held by the Court applicable to matters of procedure. But in the exercise of this high power, we must be ever on our guard, lest we erect our prejudices into legal principles. If we would guide by the light of reason, we must let our minds be bold."

To "guide by the light of reason" might well sum up the Brandeisian judicial philosophy. The Constitution was not a straightjacket but a flexible instrument that allowed people to govern themselves democratically. The Court interpreted the Constitution, and to do so properly it had to take into account not only legal precedents but common sense and social realities. For the Court to guide well its members had to be educated and then in turn educate others. As a member of the Court Brandeis used his opinions and dissents to teach his colleagues and the public that law must be related to life.

Brandeis's role on the Court was frankly educational, and so it was never enough that he declare his opinion; he had to explain it. He believed the Court had no business invalidating laws that legislatures, in their wisdom, had deemed necessary, except in clear cases of unconstitutionality. When his conservative brethren, however, insisted on interposing their own views of good and bad, he went to great lengths to explain just why the legislature had thought the statute in question necessary. He wanted to put life into the law, to make the Court relevant to the society in which it operated. Occasionally some of his admirers wondered whether he overdid it. "If you could hint to Brandeis," one friend wrote to Holmes, "that judicial opinions aren't to be written in the form of a brief it would be a great relief to the world." Although Holmes agreed, there was little he could do.

Holmes was, at times, a minor trial of sorts to Brandeis. Since his days as a law student Brandeis had admired Holmes and had considered him one of the great forces at work in rejuvenating the law. It had been Holmes who had once declared that the man of the future in law would be the "man of statistics and the master of economics," an excellent prediction of the Brandeisian type of lawyer. Yet Holmes despised facts and economically was extremely naive. "I prefer the abstract," he wrote. "Brandeis has an insatiable appetite for facts and . . . I hate them except as pegs for generalizations, but I admire the gift and wish I had a barn in which I could store them for use at need. I hope they manure my soil but they disappear in specie as soon as taken." Brandeis unsuccessfully tried to get his colleague to see the light. "Talking with Brandeis yesterday," Holmes reported, "he drove a harpoon into my midriff by saying that it would be for the good of my soul to devote my next leisure to the study of some domain of fact — suggesting the textile industry, which, after reading many reports &c, I could make living to myself by a visit to Lawrence. . . . Well, I hate facts." On this occasion, at least, Brandeis had his way, and Holmes packed off a government report with him on summer vacation; it would be the last time. The next summer he gratefully confessed that "in consideration of my age and moral infirmities, [Brandeis] absolved me from facts for the vacation and allowed me my customary sport with ideas."

While close friends as well as colleagues, the two men differed in their judicial philosophies. Holmes was Olympian in his aloofness, a liberal by negation. He would not interfere with the rights of legislatures because he would not interfere with the cosmos. Many of his dissents in support of social legislation bear an attitude almost of disdain. He once described his general philosophy to a friend: "Long ago I decided that I was not God. When a state came in here and wanted to build a slaughter house, I looked at the Constitution and if I couldn't find anything in there that said a state couldn't build a slaughter house I said to myself, if they want to build a slaughter house, God-dammit, let them build it." Despite his reputation as a great liberal, there were many inconsistencies and lapses in his writings.

Brandeis was a liberal by affirmation and championed his causes out of strong beliefs. A Jeffersonian democrat who passionately feared the curse of bigness, he fought for the rights of states to use their police powers effectively and experimentally in order to preserve a federal system he considered essential for a democratic society. "The attainment of our American ideals," he declared, "is impossible unless the states guard jealously their field of governmental action and perform zealously their appropriate duties."

In a period of transition in which the United States was turning into a great industrial power, Brandeis realized that the law would also have to adapt, that it would have to keep pace with the new society. At the same time he still believed in the old principles and ideals. In his judicial writings he time and again showed how the old faiths could be adapted to newer times. His heavily documented opinions were essential to providing a guide for American law on how to adjust to new conditions without forsaking old beliefs.

IX

Activism and Surrogates

For MOST MEN the work of the Supreme Court would be an all-consuming task. Certainly Louis Brandeis devoted great care and much time to his administrative assignments, to researching his massively documented opinions, and to writing and rewriting his statements until they became the standard of judicial craftsmanship. Because he often stood in a minority, he put even more effort into his dissents, in an effort to educate and convince the public. Yet in the quarter century of his life after his appointment, Brandeis's immense energies could not be contained within the confines of the Court.

The consequences of his early nonjudicial activities led him to adopt a strategy of working through surrogates and limiting his direct involvement to one or two tasks considered legitimate for judges; in later years he would also respond when unprecedented dangers faced the Jewish people and Palestine. His interest in legal education, for example, had always been an overriding concern, and he played an important though quiet role in upgrading the University of Louisville and its law school and also Harvard Law School. Here he set the pattern of using surrogates to act for him while he provided encouragement, ideas, and occasionally funds.

The University of Louisville had long been a modest school without great distinction, catering primarily to local students. In the American educational scene of the early 1920s, education, like other aspects of society, was dominated by giants, large prestigious schools such as Harvard and Yale whose influence extended far beyond the confines of Cambridge and New Haven. They attracted the best students and the wealthiest donors, while smaller schools tried, usually in vain, to emulate their programs, to become miniature Harvards-by-the-Maumee.

For Brandeis smallness could be as much of a virtue in education as it was in business. Local schools should not attempt to ape the big universities; instead, they should develop their own excellence and meet the specific needs of their communities. Local citizens, instead of endowing chairs at faraway universities, should work to build up the resources of nearby colleges, supporting good education within the community. Louisville, where he had been born and where he still had family, and which he always held in great affection, would be the test case, the model for local development.

For the most part he worked through his brother Alfred and Alfred's family, and he reminded them that the "Brandeis family for nearly three-quarters of a century has stood in Louisville for culture, and, at least in Uncle Lewis [Dembitz], for learning." They were to set the standard for involvement, each one assuming responsibility for a specific area and working to build up both quality and resources. Alfred would take Kentuckiana; Adele Brandeis, sociology and economics; and her sister Fanny, art and music. "If we elders have ten years to work in," he predicted, "the preliminary work will be done. The rest can be left wholly to your descendents and the Centuries."

Brandeis's own role remained quiet and behind-the-scenes. On his yearly trips to Louisville he met local businessmen and community leaders, urging them to take pride in their school and to work for its development. But he cautioned his niece not to let his name "creep in." Through Alfred he donated a substantial portion of his personal library, with its matchless collection of government and industrial documents, and provided the money to pay for cataloguing and binding. He kept a close eye on the project, bombarding Alfred and his nieces with letters, suggesting the acquisition of specific items, and identifying people who could aid them.

The one aspect that Brandeis handled directly involved the law school, where he worked closely with Dean Robert N. Miller, who had been a classmate of Felix Frankfurter's at Harvard Law. Brandeis arranged for Mr. Justice Sanford to donate his set of records and briefs to Louisville. In honor of previous Kentuckians who had served on the Supreme Court — Thomas Todd, Robert Trumble, Samuel F. Miller, and John Harlan — Brandeis donated funds to secure a full set of *Supreme Court Reports,* to be inscribed as a memorial to these men. Similarly, he provided funds to complete the *Federal Reporter* to commemorate lower court judges from Kentucky; and to honor those natives who had served as United States Attorneys General, he arranged for a full set of the Attorney General *Opinions.*

Brandeis consulted frequently with Miller on matters ranging from curriculum to staffing. He was even willing to allow the new law school building to be named in his honor, since Louisville leaders had persuaded him that such a gesture would do much in winning public interest and support. By then, however, the Court's invalidation of several major New Deal programs had engendered such controversy that he withdrew his permission, on the grounds that with the Court so much in the news he feared to do anything that might be misinterpreted by the Court's adversaries. He left his private papers to the law school, and upon his death his ashes were placed under a plaque on the veranda of the building that had nearly borne his name.

His description of what he hoped to build at Louisville bore a striking resemblance to the Harvard Law School of the 1870s where Brandeis had studied and to which he remained dedicated all his life. That school had been small, intimate, innovative, and possessed of an extraordinarily fine staff, and it had built up one of the finest law libraries in the country. Brandeis had taught there for a while, and at one time had given much thought and anguish to the choice between practice and teaching. During his more than three decades of practice in Boston, he had taken a number of promising law school graduates into his firm, and he kept in constant touch with the school's affairs. Through all his years on the Court he retained this keen interest in matters affecting Harvard, and to honor the justice's seventieth birthday in 1926, his friends could think of no more fitting a present than to donate $50,000 to the law school to establish the Brandeis Research Fellowship.

Nearly every facet of life and business at the law school came under Brandeis's scrutiny. What were the students studying? Who taught the courses? What questions did the faculty ask on final examinations? Frankfurter regularly supplied him with information, even sending him copies of tests from time to time. After perusing one batch of exam questions, Brandeis remarked gratefully that it was a good thing that Supreme Court justices did not have to take further tests once on the bench.

In the 1920s the Harvard Law School confronted burgeoning enrollments and pressures for growth. The dean, Roscoe Pound, viewed the situation as a heaven-sent opportunity to expand the student body, the physical plant, and the endowment, and to secure Harvard's reputation as the biggest and best law school in the country. Brandeis opposed such expansion from the start, seeing bigness, even at Harvard, as an unmitigated evil. Students had to be taught how to think in legal terms, a process that just could not take place in a large, impersonal academy. After Pound had personally outlined his plan to the justice in October 1924, Brandeis wrote to Frankfurter, who headed the faculty opposition to Pound's proposal: "Make frank recognition of the fact that numbers in excess of 1,000, and the proposed 350 seat lecture halls and lectures, are irreconcilable with H.L.S. traditions and aims." Brandeis discussed his reaction to the Pound proposal with the two other Harvard Law School alumni on the Supreme Court, Oliver Wendell Holmes and Edward T. Sanford, as well as with some of the lower court judges, such as Julian

Mack and Augustus Hand, nearly all of whom reacted negatively to drastic changes in the traditional Harvard approach.

As usual, once Brandeis saw a problem he proposed a solution, although in this case a rather idealistic one. Instead of expanding, Harvard Law School should become a "mother of law schools" in the same way that Harvard College had been a mother of colleges in the nineteenth century. Harvard should "make frank avowal of [its] purpose in building up the lesser schools. Then aid in placing H.L.S. resources at their disposal so far as possible." Above all, Brandeis told Zechariah Chafee, keep the law school small, and remember Goethe's line: "It is in restraint that the master primarily reveals himself." What Brandeis wanted, as he put it, was not a larger Harvard Law School, but twenty Harvard Law Schools.

Legal education, in its broadest sense, also required collaboration between the courts and the law schools. The schools not only had to educate would-be attorneys in the facts of life and law but also had to serve as watchdogs of the judicial process. Brandeis applauded at length articles that were constructively critical of the Court and its decisions and that began to appear with increasing frequency in law school journals in the 1920s. Brandeis read the law reviews carefully, often inquiring about writers of certain pieces that had caught his eye; moreover, and at that time an innovation, he cited law review articles in his decisions. This step, he explained, ought to encourage the writers to see that well-researched articles and notes did have an impact. He felt that serious and well-considered questions and criticisms coming from the law schools could not be ignored. The law schools thus became a central feature in his vision of legal education.

Other old interests continued to hold Brandeis's attention after he took his seat on the Court. Savings bank life insurance, for example, remained the reform in which he took the most pride, and as the system grew, he frequently showed visitors the quarterly reports in a manner akin to a new father displaying pictures of his offspring. His former secretary,

Alice H. Grady, became deputy secretary for savings bank insurance, and she consulted the justice whenever the commercial companies attempted to hamstring the program. At one point in the 1920s, she had a movie made to promote savings bank insurance and managed to get Brandeis to make a brief appearance in it. Afteward he commented that only for Miss Grady and savings bank insurance would he have done such a thing.

Undoubtedly the enterprise that took more of his time, thought, and money than did anything else was the rebuilding of a Jewish home in Palestine. The ouster in 1921 of the Brandeis-Mack leadership from the Zionist Organization of America left a permanently bitter taste in Brandeis's mouth; to the end of his days he believed Chaim Weizmann and Louis Lipsky to be untrustworthy, and he refused to deal with them or "their ilk." In the 1920s ZOA membership plummeted, and the irresponsible fiscal habits of the Lipsky regime ran up debts for the organization of hundreds of thousands of dollars. Lipsky padded the Zionist payroll with his cronies and used Zionist funds to make private loans to his friends. Only Hadassah, which broke with the ZOA leadership, built up membership and programs, and its leaders consulted frequently with Brandeis and his associates. Through Hadassah Brandeis provided the money for a demonstration project in the Galilee that proved that malaria in Palestine could be eradicated.

The Brandeis group, as he reminded his followers, had not resigned from Zionism but only from an administration whose principles they could not support. "We are from now on to free ourselves from all entanglements in order that we may the sooner accomplish our end," that of creating a Jewish homeland in Palestine. To further this goal, the Brandeis-Mack faction established the Palestine Endowment Fund and the Palestine Development Council (PDC), the former handling donations while the latter was to channel investment monies into desirable projects in Palestine. Here Brandeis stood true to his principles that donations and investments should not be commingled; as Felix Frankfurter pointed out, in fiscal affairs Brandeis was as conservative as any banker. His opponents, however, saw the PDC as a device to foist private enterprise capitalism on the young settlement, and Weizmann to the end of his life charged Brandeis with opposing social progress in Palestine, of trying to create a capitalist society at the expense of Jewish values. In truth, the Endowment Fund and the PDC represented that balance Brandeis so cherished: investment capital for economic growth, with donation funds for those projects which would not attract investment but which were socially necessary.

Despite much time and effort, the two undertakings never achieved the results Brandeis desired. Working outside the Zionist organization, without the benefit of a large propaganda apparatus or membership infrastructure by which they could have reached masses of people, they were doomed to depend upon a few wealthy donors. The Brandeis-Mack group totally misjudged the willingness of small businessmen to put their money into Palestinian projects. Even when worthwhile and attractive endeavors came along, the PDC lacked the resources to undertake them. The Rutenberg hydroelectric scheme, which ultimately developed into Palestine's power grid, first turned to the Brandeis group for financing, but after extensive consultations the PDC admitted it did not have enough investors to underwrite the important and potentially remunerative venture. In the end the PDC merged into the Palestine Economic Corporation founded by the Marshall group and the Joint Distribution Committee. The Palestine Endowment Fund eventually succeeded on a modest scale, and its trust funds were to prove an important resource in the growth of the Hebrew University in Jerusalem.

The economic cooperation with the Marshall group, a program begun after the war and interrupted by the Cleveland schism, marked the beginning of the Brandeis-Mack group's return to power in the Zionist movement. As the 1920s wore on, more and more members of the rank and file called for the justice's return. For Brandeis the status of ZOA affairs elicited nothing but contempt. When Charles Cowen visited him to discuss Zionist affairs, Brandeis vented his anger: "I spoke to him impressively and torrentially of the shame to the Jewish people which had come from this self-seeking, incompetent and dishonest [Lipsky] administration, which had prostituted a great cause; which, enjoying fat salaries in New York, had let school teachers in Palestine starve with six months of salaries in arrears; which had defied the teachings of the prophets that had sustained and maintained the Jewish People throughout the centuries." When Cowen feebly asked what should be done, Brandeis drew the cloak of Isaiah around him and declared: "Return to truth, put an end to the lying. Turn out those who have obtained money under false pretenses and misappropriated that which they secured."

At almost any time after 1927 Brandeis could have regained control of the ZOA had he been willing to assume personal leadership of the organization. But by now he was over seventy and believed that an official position with the ZOA would be incompatible with his duties on the Court. He wanted his group back in power, his principles guiding the movement; but none of his associates, not even Julian Mack or Stephen Wise, had his prestige. They did, however, have the experience of numerous reform battles, and as the ZOA continued to deteriorate, the Brandeis group brought that experience into play.

The campaign to oust the Lipsky administration bore all the marks of classic progressive battles for civic reform: exposure of the crooks, organization of the citizenry, and ultimate control of the political apparatus; and there was no doubt about who engineered the drive. In a series of well-publicized moves Zionist leaders who had earlier agreed to cooperate with Lipsky now resigned to join the opposition; Hadassah, the largest Zionist group in the country, added its potent voice to the chorus of criticism. Under pressure, Chaim Weizmann reluctantly appointed a committee to investigate charges of financial mismanagement by Lipsky. Its audit, while not proving malfeasance, showed Lipsky and his aides to have been at the least misfeasant, with the result that tens of thousands of dollars had been wasted or misspent. In March 1929 Chaim Arlosoroff, the brilliant theoretician of Labor Zionism, released a forty-eight-page analysis of the ZOA in which he predicted an imminent "political, moral and organizational breakdown of the American Zionist movement" unless there were changes in the leadership. The final impetus came when Arab riots in Palestine at the end of the summer left 133 Jews dead and more than 400 injured. The lame response of Zionist leaders both in New York and London led to an irresistible demand by the membership for change.

In the spring of 1930, after several months of negotiation, the Brandeis-Mack group returned to head the Zionist Organization of America. Although Lipsky and his followers received token seats on the executive and administrative committees, power rested with Brandeis and his lieutenants, his surrogates, especially Robert Szold, who took direct charge of the organization and worked valiantly to restore its nearly moribund finances. Brandeis's role in the Zionist movement from 1930 until his death would be the same: streams of advice to Szold, Neumann, Wise, and others who held formal office; generous contributions of money for emergency purposes; an emphasis on practical economic work rather than propaganda; and rarely, but usually effectively, personal intervention in a crisis.

Although Brandeis worked through many people, undoubtedly his most important surrogate was Professor Felix Frankfurter of the Harvard Law School. He had first met Frankfurter when the latter had served as an assistant to Secretary of War Henry L. Stimson in the Taft administration, and in 1914 Brandeis was instrumental in convincing Frankfurter to accept an appointment to the Harvard faculty. During the First World War Frankfurter had returned to Washington as head of the War Labor Policies Board and had also been part of the Brandeis group in the ZOA. At the Paris Peace Conference the Harvard professor had drafted nearly all the legal memoranda that the Zionists had presented to the heads of state and the various commissions. Like Brandeis, Frankfurter believed in a living law, and after 1916 he had become the leading practitioner of the Brandeis brief in such matters as the Washington *Minimum Wage* case.

During the 1920s and 1930s Frankfurter served as a conduit for funneling information from a variety of reform groups to Brandeis, advising him of their problems and progress and in turn conveying his advice. Brandeis recognized that on a professor's salary Frankfurter could never be as free as he himself had been, so he set up a private fund for Frankfurter to use in reform work in order that he would not have to turn away from a worthy cause because of lack of money. Brandeis, who as a judge refused to intervene in the Sacco-Vanzetti case, in fact financed the work of the two anarchists' leading defender.

Frankfurter, whom Brandeis once revealingly described as "half brother, half son," also proved a unique outlet for Brandeis's views. In the early 1920s Frankfurter served as a contributing editor on the *New Republic* and arranged for a number of unsigned pieces to appear on different industrial and social issues. The author of these works obviously felt he could not publish them under his own name, lest his objectivity as a Supreme Court justice be impaired. In addition, in order to explain some of the Court's rulings or his own dissents to the public, Brandeis briefed Frankfurter on some cases, and the Harvard professor then published these explications under his own name in the journal. This fruitful relationship brought Brandeis much private satisfaction, as did his other work with young people. He knew that his ideas would live on only if another generation picked up the battle for reform. And in the 1930s the opportunity for reviving the reform impulse appeared greater than it had been in nearly a generation.

X

"Isaiah"

"I think a general business depression is beginning," Brandeis wrote on November 13, 1929, his seventy-third birthday. Two weeks earlier the stock market had plummeted, ushering in the most severe economic collapse in the nation's history. "Speculation has been so widespread," Brandeis continued, "that it affects directly a much larger percentage of the population than any earlier era; and luxuries have formed a much larger percentage of the total expenditures than ever before. Moreover, our productive capacity has never before exceeded so largely our capacity to consume. The percentage of our exports is bound to shrink with the European recovery and development."

For more than a quarter century he had warned about the danger of economic concentration, but in the heyday of Republican prosperity few people had paid much attention to him. The Depression brought a new popularity to Brandeis's economic philosophy; *Business — A Profession* and *Other People's Money* were reissued in inexpensive editions, and an anthology of his writings appeared, together with numerous biographical sketches. Frequently his mail brought him hosannas from people who suddenly appreciated his views on the curse of bigness.

Brandeis's last years saw the nation and the world reel from one crisis to another. The social and economic optimism of the 1920s, a decade of seemingly eternal prosperity, gave way to the disillusion and grinding poverty of the 1930s. The old gods had died, and with them went the last remnants of American innocence and naivete. The New Deal of Franklin D. Roosevelt experimented boldly, but failure in one area often accompanied success in another, and the nation did not recover economically until armament orders flooded American factories and the draft dried up the unemployment pool. Overseas, fascism rose to power in Germany, turning that bastion of *Kultur* into an ugly, hateful killing machine, while indecision paralyzed the Western democracies. In Palestine Zionists feared their years of labor would go for naught as Great Britain reneged on the Balfour promise. And in his eighty-third year Brandeis saw the world go to war, a conflict more terrible than the civil strife of his childhood or the European war of his middle years.

Through it all he maintained his serenity, his belief that ultimately goodness and reason would triumph. He continued apace with all his former activities, writing opinions and dissents on the Court, directing Zionist activities after his backers had regained control of the ZOA, conferring with government leaders and bureaucrats, and, behind the scenes, attempting to influence the policies of the Roosevelt administration. There he stood, seemingly above the chaos, his white hair completing the portrait of a prophet, the man to whom Roosevelt aptly referred as "Isaiah."

The New Deal presented problems as well as opportunities. From the beginning Brandeis had taken Roosevelt seriously, unlike many other former progressives or even Justice Holmes, who once characterized Roosevelt as "a second-class intellect, but a first-rate temperament." Undoubtedly much of Brandeis's favorable impression derived from reports by Felix Frankfurter, who had established close ties with Roosevelt while the latter had been governor of New York, and from his nephew Louis B. Wehle, who had long been a Roosevelt enthusiast. At Frankfurter's urgings the White House made contact with him early in the New Deal. From mid-1933 until his death Brandeis had access to the president, who sought his views directly and indirectly through such intermediaries as Frankfurter and journalist Norman Hapgood.

Roosevelt, however, was inundated with advice from many quarters. Advocates of Theodore Roosevelt's New Nationalism called upon the new administration to combat the Depression by fostering nationalistic economic consolidation and cooperation under government supervision and ending, once and for all, the illusion that competition fostered prosperity. Unhampered competition in the 1920s, they argued, had been the primary cause of the nation's economic woes. These New Nationalists used the analogy of the First World War as their model. During wartime the government had allowed industries to coordinate their activities under the aegis of the War Industries Board; as a result production had shot up, labor conditions had improved, and this cooperative effort had unified the nation. Roosevelt himself described the Depression as an emergency as grave as war itself; the proper response should therefore be the same as when the nation had actually gone to war, with cooperation replacing competition.

The old Wilsonians, chief among them Brandeis, stood unalterably opposed to this concept. For them the 1920s had been marked not by true competition but by economic consolidation, stock manipulation, and the growth of holding companies, the worst form of monopoly. So long as economic power remained in the hands of the few, the nation would enjoy neither equitably distributed property nor industrial democracy. Bigness had proven to be a curse in the 1920s, and the answer lay not in more bigness but in less; not only industry but government itself had to be smaller. While the federal government undoubtedly had a role to play in recovery, as many duties as possible should devolve upon the states.

During the early years of the New Deal the former New Nationalists carried the day, and the National Recovery Administration (NRA) as well as the Agricultural Adjustment Agency (AAA) epitomized the ideals of the central planners, while the Glass-Steagel and Security Regulations Acts provided the federal government with a watchdog role, protecting the public. Old-line Bull Moose progressives such as William Allen White and Harold Ickes were absolutely delighted with this Democratic Roosevelt. More important, they claimed that their programs were working; by July 1933 the factory production index had climbed from 56 to 101, and industrial stocks from 63 to 109. Enthusiasm abounded as tens of thousands marched in parades behind the NRA's Blue Eagle; industries lined up to sign codes that promised to abolish child labor and provide union recognition and collective bargaining.

The consolidationists were not without their critics, and perhaps none was more effective than Louis Brandeis. Through Frankfurter he had access to many agency officials. At his weekly teas Brandeis propounded his views on the evils of bigness in government as well as in business, and he urged his admirers to work in their own fields for the preservation of the old verities. Nor did Isaiah stop at the lower echelons; he knew and saw many of the cabinet members and agency heads, and he argued his case with the president himself.

The curbing of bigness, he wrote, "is indispensable to true Democracy and Liberty. It is the very foundation also of wisdom in things human. 'Nothing too much.' I hope you can make your progressives see this truth. If they don't, we may get amelioration, but not a working 'New Deal.' And we are apt to get Fascist manifestations. Remember the inevitable ineffectiveness of regulation, i.e., the limits of efficiency in regulation. If the Lord had intended things to be big, he would have made man bigger — in brains and character."

Brandeis already had a model in mind of the efficacy of energetic response to the crisis on the state level. In Wisconsin his daughter Elizabeth and her husband Paul Raushenbush, together with Harold Groves and Governor Philip LaFollette, had enacted a pioneering unemployment compensation law in January 1932. The heart of the plan was an experience rating under which the size of the employer's contribution was determined by previous success or failure in maintaining workers on the job, an idea that directly reflected Brandeis's long-time concern with regularity of employment. Thus those companies with the highest unemployment paid the most, while those maintaining their work force paid the least.

Brandeis had been concerned about the effects of erratic and undependable job conditions since his days as counsel to the Filene brothers and the McElwain shoe company; it had been a factor in the garment industry protocol; and during the 1920s he had consistently urged Paul U. Kellogg and the *Survey* associates to publicize the benefits, to workers and employers alike, of stabilized working conditions. Now with 13 million workers unemployed the problem took on new urgency. The Wisconsin plan throughout remained his model for state action; the problem would be to ensure uniformity in the different states without a federal takeover.

Although the Wisconsin plan had many supporters, several economists questioned whether it was the proper model for national action. Here was a major dilemma of the New Deal: Could one really deal with a national emergency on a state level, or did one have to develop a comprehensive and unified program? Paul Douglas, then a professor at the University of Chicago, argued that mass unemployment, created by conditions beyond the control of a single company or a single state, required an overall rather than a piecemeal solution. While the states could serve as social laboratories, it did not necessarily follow that a plan that succeeded in one state would be as efficacious in other states or in the entire country. A national system would facilitate collection of taxes, simplify administration, and ensure equitable distribution. In the end, as occurred with so much New Deal legislation, the administration adopted a compromise measure that tried to keep everyone happy. The Social Security system would be national, but unemployment compensation would be left to the states. The merit rating remained, but the new system allowed for such divergences as to penalize states that tried to provide more generous benefits. Brandeis viewed the final version of the bill as a mixed blessing; while it carried out some of his ideas, it still retained, in his view, too large a role for the federal government.

Brandeis, of course, had one other forum in which he could protest. On April 22, 1934, he wrote to his daughter: "I see little to be joyous about in the New Deal measures most talked about; NRA and AAA seem to be going from bad to worse." Both laws eventually came before the United States Supreme Court, and although Brandeis differed sharply with the consolidationist philosophy behind the measures, as a jurist he proved able to distinguish between what he liked and what he considered constitutional. The NRA reached the Court first, and the *Schechter* case exposed all the weaknesses of the program. A unanimous Court, speaking through Chief Justice Hughes, invalidated the law, declaring that it far exceeded the limits of the government's commerce powers. In a concurring opinion Mr. Justice Cardozo called the sweeping grants of legislative power "delegation running riot." A stunned Roosevelt could not believe that the entire Court had gone against him, knocking out what had been the centerpiece of New Deal reform. "What about old Isaiah?" he asked. To the press he declared that the decision relegated the nation to "the horse-and-buggy definition of interstate commerce." In fact, the administration had now paid the price for its hastiness, its efforts to write in something for everyone, with a resultant shoddiness in drafting the bill that particularly affronted Brandeis.

That same day, May 27, 1935, the Court also struck down the Frazier-Lemke Act, a measure that provided relief for mortgagers and for which Brandeis had great sympathy. This act, too, had been poorly drawn. Speaking for a unanimous Court, Brandeis declared that private property retained constitutional protection even when severe economic conditions clothed it with a public interest. "If the public interest requires, and permits, the taking of property of individual mortgagees in order to relieve the necessities of individual mortgagors, resort must be had to proceedings by eminent domain; so that through taxation, the burden of the relief

afforded in the public interest may be borne by the public."
The public interest was indeed paramount, but democracy
could not survive, even in crises, unless the rights of the
minority received full constitutional protection.

All in all, however, Brandeis voted against specific New
Deal measures only three times: in the *Schechter* case, in the
Panama Oil decision, which repudiated a section of the
National Industrial Recovery Act, and in the *Radford* case,
which struck down the Frazier-Lemke Act. But the *Butler*
decision in early 1936 contained an equally wretched majority
opinion for the Court. Speaking through Mr. Justice Roberts,
six jurists condemned the AAA processing tax as illegitimate,
a subterfuge for the "expropriation of money from one
group for the benefit of another." Roberts disingenuously
announced that the Court never questioned the legislative
wisdom of a proposal but merely laid the law alongside the
Constitution to see if the two squared off. Here indeed was a
"horse-and-buggy" decision, and Brandeis, despite whatever
reservation he may have had about the program, joined with
Cardozo in backing Harlan Fiske Stone's brilliant and biting
dissent.

The demise of the NRA and the AAA marked the end of
the first New Deal, that part of Roosevelt's administration
characterized by measures derived from the New Nationalism. Roosevelt, however, had already begun to move in a new
direction, influenced by growing pressures from the Left and
by the lack of cooperation he perceived among businessmen.
Industrialists were willing to accept the benefits of the NRA
but not pass them on to the consumer or recognize the right
of labor to organize. The creation of the reactionary Liberty
League in 1934 only reinforced Roosevelt's view, one definitely shared by Brandeis, that there could be no compromise between the interests of the public and those of big business.

Starting in 1934 Roosevelt proposed a series of measures
that definitely reflected the ideas of Brandeis, Felix Frankfurter, and their allies. Planning gave way to reform, and the

administration sponsored a number of bills, all bearing hall-marks of the Brandeisian philosophy and all carefully drawn with an eye to judicial review. The Public Utilities Holding Company Act broke up pyramided trusts; the Banking Act of 1935 greatly strengthened the regulatory power of the Federal Reserve system; the Wagner-Lewis Act embodied in part the Wisconsin plan; and under Thurman Arnold the Justice Department began a sweeping attack on monopolies. The Wagner Act created a National Labor Relations Board and gave labor the right to unionize and to bargain collectively, powers the Brandeisians saw as necessary to balance industrial might; the Wealth Tax Act, although it did not go as far as Brandeis wanted, was a major conceptual step toward breaking up great concentrations of wealth. Moreover, some of the better provisions of the NRA were resurrected. The Walsh-Healy Act required federal contractors to observe minimum labor standards, while the Robinson-Patman Act eliminated some of the purchasing advantages of chain stores. The Miller-Tydings Act also embodied a Brandeisian principle in strengthening fair-trade laws. Through it all Brandeis kept a careful eye on details, prodding here, encouraging there, letting Roosevelt know that at last he was on the right track.

The difference between the first and the second New Deals lay more in tone and style than in substance. Although planners appeared to have been in the ascendancy in the early months of the New Deal, Roosevelt at no time seriously considered the creation of a planned economy. The rise to power of Felix Frankfurter and the neo-Brandeisians represented a shift in political style more than in ideology. There is doubt that Roosevelt really understood the Brandeisian philosophy, although he once declared that "Brandeis is one thousand percent right in principle."

Both New Deals derived almost entirely from ideas proposed by progressives nearly a generation before. Even the planning-oriented Tennessee Valley Authority had numerous antecedents in the work of George Norris and others;

Brandeis himself had suggested a similar program for Alaskan development in 1911. Lines connecting Franklin Roosevelt's New Deal with the earlier progressives were clear, and contradictions within the New Deal reflected perfectly contradictions inherent in progressivism itself. Franklin Roosevelt, like his cousin Theodore and Woodrow Wilson, believed in preserving a capitalist economy, but one that controlled the abuses of big business and rectified some of the inequities. This goal, if not all the New Deal's methods, Louis Brandeis could endorse.

Brandeis understood that Roosevelt's instincts for the most part remained basically decent; that in conditions similar to those that had brought Hitler and Mussolini to power on the continent, Roosevelt had remained committed to democratic government. Moreover, Brandeis's experience as a reformer, stretching back more than four decades, gave him a clearer view of the pressures on the president. The determined opposition of business leaders and the obtuseness of conservatives often forced Roosevelt to take more extreme positions than he had originally planned. Understanding the situation, following these twists and turns, Brandeis was sympathetic to Roosevelt even when disagreeing with him. But when the president employed deceit, the aging jurist vigorously opposed him.

After knocking out the NRA and AAA, the Supreme Court had gone on to find one administration bill after another unconstitutional. The five-man conservative majority now opposed reform not only by the national government but by the states as well. Not since the turn of the century had the Court stood so opposed to popular and legislative will. Roosevelt, fighting desperately to bring the nation out of its worst economic crisis, saw his entire legislative program threatened. Under the guise of reforming the Court, he introduced a bill in February 1937 to pack the tribunal with up to six more judges, enough to provide a comfortable majority favorable to New Deal legislation.

The episode displayed the opportunism of the Roosevelt

administration at its worst. Had the president at least been candid enough to present his case as an effort to carry through a program overwhelmingly endorsed by the voters in the 1936 election, he might have gained some support. But the blatant duplicity of his argument that all he wanted to do was relieve court congestion gave anti–New Dealers a rallying point. Even liberals supporting reform did not want to tamper with the Supreme Court.

No one doubted where Brandeis stood. His law clerk at the time, Willard Hurst, noted that the justice disliked the "smart" or the "clever" in public business. He resolutely opposed the president's plan, and while maintaining his customary public reticence about political matters, Brandeis let his feelings be known. Mrs. Brandeis called upon the daughter of Senator Burton K. Wheeler, an old progressive warhorse who was leading the fight against the president's bill. As she left she declared: "You tell your obstinate father we think he is making a courageous fight." Wheeler soon called upon Brandeis and asked him about the real state of the Court's business. Were the justices overworked and behind schedule? Was there a delay in handling important cases? Brandeis suggested that these questions be addressed to Chief Justice Hughes. When Wheeler said he did not know Hughes, Brandeis responded that the "Chief Justice knows you, and what you're doing," and he firmly led the senator to the telephone.

The result was a letter from Hughes to Wheeler, pointing out in detail that the Supreme Court was fully abreast of its work, with the justices performing their duties efficiently and in good order. Although Hughes had been unable to contact all his colleagues over the weekend, he had secured the assent of Willis Van Devanter, one of the conservatives, and of Brandeis, a member of the liberal minority. The reading of this letter marked the end of the court-packing bill, and on July 22, after more than five months of bitter struggle, the Senate recommitted the bill.

Afterward Roosevelt claimed that he had lost the battle but won the campaign. During the debate Justice Willis Van De-

vanter resigned, allowing Roosevelt to nominate liberal Hugo
Black; within thirty months the president replaced four more
judges, ensuring a Court favorable to his reform legislation.
Meanwhile, concerned over the furor created by the split
decisions, Mr. Justice Roberts switched his vote in several key
cases, thus handing the administration further victories. Yet
Roosevelt may have ultimately lost the war, for the Court fight
fractured the unity of the Democratic party and provided a
nucleus around which an anti–New Deal coalition formed,
preventing the passage of any major reform legislation in
Roosevelt's second term.

The outcome of the battle, the preservation of the Court's
integrity, pleased Brandeis. Whether as a critic of judicial
obtuseness or as a member of the Court's liberal minority, he
had always argued for an independent judiciary. The answer
to the problems of a Court disconnected from social and
economic realities lay in education, not in shortsighted expe-
dients. In fact, Brandeis's own efforts to educate his brethren
had already begun to pay dividends.

Brandeis's championing of free speech in the 1920s laid the
groundwork for broadening this liberty in the 1930s. The
Court, led by Hughes, interpreted the due process clause of
the Fourteenth Amendment to include freedom of speech
and press while invalidating several state laws passed during
the postwar nativist hysteria. The prudent investment theory
of valuation, set forth by Brandeis in a 1923 dissent, became
constitutional doctrine a decade later, much to the joy of
public utilities hard hit by the Depression. In 1937 the Court
reversed itself and upheld an act forbidding wiretapping by
federal officers.

The most impressive results of Brandeis's long educational
campaign affected labor, an area in which Brandeis had
raised his first lance in 1907 in the *Muller* case. The use of
injunctions in labor disputes, a weapon so dear to conservatives, finally came under state and federal restrictions that a
majority of the Court upheld. The Norris-LaGuardia Act of
1932 repudiated the yellow-dog contract, in which workers

had to promise not to join unions, while the National Labor Relations Act of 1935 embodied Brandeis's dissents in the *Hitchman, Duplex Printing,* and other cases. In the *Jones & Laughlin* case, which upheld the law, Chief Justice Hughes in one sentence summed up what Brandeis had been preaching for so many years: "We refuse to shut our eyes to the plainest facts of our national life and to deal with these issues in an intellectual vacuum." Perhaps the greatest victory came in 1937, when Brandeis's arguments as an attorney in the 1914 *O'Hara* case finally became the law of the land; in *West Coast Hotel* v. *Parrish* the Supreme Court upheld the validity of minimum wage legislation. The great dissenter had become the prophet of a living law.

Faith in education as a cure for social ills or judicial ignorance, however, presupposes a sane universe. Brandeis once told his daughter Susan that "if you will just start with the idea that this is a hard world, it will all be much simpler." Yet while Brandeis expected life to be hard, he also expected it to be rational. Difficulties existed to be overcome by hard work and talent; problems were there to test an individual's abilities. Brandeis gloried in the battles of life, but he assumed that rules existed, with rewards and punishments appropriate to the deeds. In the 1930s these assumptions so dear to the progressive mind yielded to madness. Hitler and the Nazis turned Germany into a charnel house where all the old verities, all the fairness and rationality and beauty of life, disappeared.

Few people in the United States took Adolf Hitler seriously, a mistake that would cost dearly later on. Even most Jewish leaders assumed that Nazism was but one more bad time in the long history of European Jewry, and that as Germany recovered economically, the anti-Jewish mania would decline. Stephen Wise almost alone saw the danger of Hitler not only to Jewry but to democracy as well. In 1933 he organized a series of protest demonstrations, and he found his old Zionist chief a source of constant encouragement and support. Brandeis recognized that German Jews faced a serious danger.

Moreover, he did not believe that the Western democracies had either the courage to confront Hitler or the compassion and generosity to take in refugees fleeing fascism. He told Wise early in 1933 that the only solution lay in a mass emigration of German Jewry, an act Brandeis believed would hurt Hitler and Germany through the loss of Jewish business skill and capital. In a sane world this might have been true, but Hitler could not have cared less about temporary economic difficulties that stood in the way of ridding Germany of Jews.

Brandeis, of course, had a plan, the massive movement of Jews from Europe to Palestine, which prospered despite the depression afflicting Western Europe and America. Now seemed the perfect opportunity to demonstrate the essential rationale of Zionism, the need for a homeland to take in Jews fleeing from persecution and danger. But once again rationality fell victim to fear. The British, after trying to placate both Arabs and Jews in the 1920s, had decided to throw in their lot with the Arabs, and they spent much of the 1930s working to abrogate the Balfour pledge and the commitment of the mandate. For Brandeis, who had, like Wise and other Zionist leaders, long been an Anglophile, Albion's perfidy hurt deeply.

There was little anyone could do in the 1930s to stop either Hitler's madness or England's treachery. On several occasions Brandeis personally went to the White House to urge President Roosevelt to use his influence with the British to keep the gates of Palestine open. A proposed white paper in 1936 severely restricting Jewish immigration to Palestine was withheld because of Roosevelt's intercession, taken at the behest of Brandeis and Stephen Wise. But Roosevelt's attention focused on domestic problems; not until later in the decade did he concern himself with foreign matters, and then mainly with defense. The president, like most Americans, had no time to spare for Jewish refugees.

Throughout these years Brandeis never wavered in his faith that Palestine would be rebuilt to become a truly Jewish homeland. He believed, perhaps naively, that ultimately the

English would come to their senses and redeem their honor. He also expected, more realistically, that eventually all American Jewry would endorse the Zionist program; after all, Louis Marshall had led his colleagues into the Jewish Agency compact, whereby the wealthier American Jews could support Palestinian development without accepting any nationalistic ideology. In the 1930s, however, the Agency non-Zionists, led by Felix Warburg, refused to fund any but the most innocuous Palestinian projects. Following the 1936 Arab riots, for example, the Haganah (Palestine Jewry's defense force) appealed to the Agency for money to buy arms. Even though Great Britain had approved the purchase of defense weapons, Warburg refused to free the money. David Ben-Gurion finally appealed to Stephen S. Wise, then president of the ZOA, who secretly sent more than $40,000, which Brandeis provided. On another occasion Brandeis put up the funds to purchase a large tract of land near the Arab port of Akaba, after Ben-Gurion explained to him that a Jewish state would need water access to the Indian Ocean for trade in the Orient; on that land Jewish settlers later built the port city of Eilat.

Eventually even prophets must succumb to the ravages of time. Brandeis carried a heavy burden of Court and extra-judicial activities well into his eighties, but the physical effects of age could not be retarded. As he once noted to his daughter, "I am as usual, but the auto men are right. Old machines are unreliable and the maintenance cost high." Ill health began to plague him in 1937, and in January 1939 he suffered a heart attack. Always a realist, he bowed to the inevitable, and on February 13, 1939, after attending to his regular Court duties, he sat down and wrote a one-sentence note to the president: "Pursuant to the Act of March 1937, I retire this day from regular active service on the bench." The entire country now joined in tribute to the man whose nomination to the Court twenty-three years earlier had caused the greatest confirmation fight the nation had ever seen. To

Brandeis's immense satisfaction, Roosevelt named William O. Douglas, chairman of the Securities Exchange Commission and a confirmed Brandeisian, to the vacant seat, joining Felix Frankfurter whom the president had appointed only a few weeks earlier.

In his remaining years Brandeis kept a constant eye on those affairs that had interested him for so many years — Zionism, savings bank insurance, and labor conditions. He continued meeting with government officials and reformers, intervening when he could on Jewish matters with Roosevelt. In the fall of 1941 his health deteriorated rapidly, and on October 1 he suffered another heart attack; four days later he quietly passed away.

Brandeis's life and career spanned more than eight decades, and he played important roles in numerous areas: legal practice, civic and industrial reform, Zionism, and jurisprudence. His most lasting contributions were the creation of an American Zionist movement and the establishment of legal bases for a truly living law. But a man's life is more than its parts; it must be judged on its wholeness, on how it was lived as well as on what was accomplished. Matthew Arnold's lines had long been Brandeis's personal philosophy: "Life is not a having and a getting, but a being and a becoming."

Parts of Brandeis's life may seem irrelevant in the 1980s. His economic doctrine flew in the face of irresistible historic forces; some of his labor theories also made more sense in the abstract than in real life. But the consistency in his career and thought transcended the momentary and the commonplace; his was a mind of one piece. His life and work displayed the highest ideals and most effective practices of the progressive tradition. Louis Brandeis dreamed dreams, but he also showed how they could be made into realities. His accomplishments both as a reformer and as a judge remain a lasting testament to that tradition.

A Note on Sources

THE MAIN SOURCE for this study is the voluminous body of Louis D. Brandeis Papers at the University of Louisville Law Library. Among the more important secondary collections are the Felix Frankfurter and Woodrow Wilson Papers at the Library of Congress; the Franklin D. Roosevelt Papers at the Roosevelt Library in Hyde Park, New York; the Stephen S. Wise Papers at the American Jewish Historical Society in Waltham, Massachusetts; and the Division of Savings Bank Insurance Archives in Boston, Massachusetts. In addition, a number of oral history memoirs at Columbia University and the Hebrew University in Jerusalem contain useful information.

Brandeis's writings are available in several volumes. Some of his progressive speeches and articles are gathered in *Business — A Profession* (Boston, 1914) and *Other People's Money and How the Bankers Use It* (New York, 1914). His Zionist statements are in Solomon Goldman, ed., *Brandeis on Zionism* (Washington, 1942); and a good overall anthology is Osmond K. Fraenkel, ed., *The Curse of Bigness* (New York, 1934). For his correspondence, see Melvin I. Urofsky and David W. Levy, eds., *Letters of Louis D. Brandeis* (five volumes, Albany, 1971–1978). The best single source for Brandeis's life is Alpheus T. Mason, *Brandeis: A Free Man's Life* (New York, 1946). Mason also wrote several other books on various episodes of Brandeis's career, including *Brandeis: Lawyer and Judge in the Modern State* (Princeton, 1933); *The Brandeis Way* (Princeton, 1938), dealing with savings bank insurance; *Bureaucracy Convicts Itself* (New York, 1941), about the Pinchot-Ballinger affair; and with Henry Lee Staples, *The Fall of a Railroad Empire* (Syracuse, 1947), on the New Haven battle. Works that correct or amplify Mason's studies include James L. Penick, Jr.,

Progressive Politics and Conservation: The Ballinger-Pinchot Affair (Chicago, 1968); Richard M. Abrams, "Brandeis and the New Haven–Boston & Maine Merger Battle Revisited," *Business History Review* 36 (1962): 408–430; and Melvin I. Urofsky, *A Mind of One Piece* (New York, 1971).

Brandeis's early career in Boston is examined in Allon Gal, *Brandeis of Boston* (Cambridge, 1979). For New England in this period see Arthur Mann, *Yankee Reformers in an Urban Age* (New York, 1966) and Richard M. Abrams, *Conservatism in a Progressive Era* (Cambridge, 1964). For changes in the legal profession and the law see James Willard Hurst, *The Growth of American Law* (Boston, 1950); Arnold M. Paul, *Conservative Crisis and the Rule of Law* (Ithaca, 1960); and Jerold Auerbach, *Unequal Justice* (New York, 1977). Background for the *Muller* case is in Chapter 13 of Josephine C. Goldmark, *Impatient Crusader; Florence Kelley's Life Story* (Urbana, Illinois, 1953); while the Brandeis briefs are available in *Women in Industry* . . . (New York, 1908) and in Josephine C. Goldmark, *Fatigue and Efficiency* (New York, 1912). For an account of his law practice see the memoir by his partner Edward F. McClennen, "Louis D. Brandeis as a Lawyer," 33 *Massachusetts Law Quarterly* 1 (1948). Brandeis University in 1979 published a microform edition of briefs and other legal documents culled from the office archives. For a broad perspective see David W. Levy, "The Lawyer as Judge: Brandeis's View of the Legal Profession," 22 *Oklahoma Law Review* 374 (1969).

A variety of books are available on progressive reform and the changing economic conditions of the country at the turn of the century. See especially Robert Wiebe, *The Search for Order, 1870–1920* (New York, 1967); Samuel P. Hays, *The Response to Industrialism, 1885–1914* (Chicago, 1957); G. Warren Nutter, *The Extent of Enterprise Monopoly in the United States, 1899–1939* (Chicago, 1951); and Sidney Fine, *Laissez-Faire and the General Welfare State* (Ann Arbor, 1956). A balanced overview is John A. Garraty, *The New Commonwealth, 1877–1890* (New York, 1968). Brandeis's attacks on monopolies are found in many places but especially in his muckraking articles in *Collier's Weekly* and in testimony before numerous congressional committees; a full listing is in Roy M. Mersky, *Louis Dembitz Brandeis, 1856–1941: A Bibliography* (New Haven, 1958), pp. 14–27. An interesting exposition of the idea that the Brandeisian approach was futile from the start can be found in Gabriel Kolko, *The Triumph of Conservatism* (New York, 1963).

Relations with Woodrow Wilson are derived from Arthur S. Link, *Wilson* (Princeton, 1947–, five volumes to date), from Link's *Woodrow Wilson and the Progressive Era* (New York, 1963), and from various biographies and manuscript collections of figures in the administration. The fight over the nomination is best handled by Mason in *A Free Man's Life*, Chapters 30–31, and by Alden Todd in *Justice on Trial* (New York, 1964). The letters written by Brandeis during the five-month struggle constitute the nearest thing we have to an autobiography and are available in Urofsky and Levy, *Letters*, 4:25–240, *passim*. One should also see U.S. Senate, *Hearings . . . on the Nomination of Louis D. Brandeis*, 64th Cong., 1st Sess. (Washington, 1916).

Material on American Zionism is becoming more plentiful, and much of it deals with Brandeis's influence. The idolatrous approach of Jacob deHaas, *Louis D. Brandeis: A Biographical Sketch* (New York, 1929), is more than compensated for in the very critical work of Yonathan Shapiro, *Leadership of the American Zionist Organization, 1897–1930* (Urbana, Illinois, 1972). See also Louis Lipsky, *A Gallery of Zionist Profiles* (New York, 1956); Stephen S. Wise, *Challenging Years* (New York, 1949); *Felix Frankfurter Reminisces* (New York, 1960); and Melvin I. Urofsky, *American Zionism from Herzl to the Holocaust* (Garden City, New York, 1975).

The literature on Brandeis as jurist is overwhelming. The extensive corpus of Brandeisian opinions, both in the majority and in dissent, is found in *United States Reports* from 1917 to 1939. Moreover, Alexander M. Bickel's *The Unpublished Opinions of Mr. Justice Brandeis* (Cambridge, Massachusetts, 1957) provides insight into research Brandeis did that never saw its way into print. For Holmes and Brandeis a useful work is Samuel J. Konefsky, *The Legacy of Holmes and Brandeis* (New York, 1956). Felix Frankfurter wrote extensively on Brandeis; see especially his "Mr. Justice Brandeis and the Constitution," 45 *Harvard Law Review* 33 (1931), and *Mr. Justice Brandeis* (New Haven, 1932), which he edited. Brandeis's former law clerks have also written at length about him. See, for example, Paul A. Freund, "Mr. Justice Brandeis: A Centennial Memoir," 70 *Harvard Law Review* 769 (1956), and "Mr. Justice Brandeis," in Allison Dunham and Philip B. Kurkland, eds., *Mr. Justice* (Chicago, 1956); see also Freund's *On Understanding the Supreme Court* (Boston, 1950). J. Willard Hurst has dealt with Brandeis in *The Growth of American Law* (Boston, 1950) and "Who is the 'Great' Appellate Judge?" 24 *Indiana Law Journal* 394 (1949). An extremely appreciative analysis is

Harold J. Laski, "Mr. Justice Brandeis," *Harper's Magazine* CLXVIII (January 1934): 209–218.

Brandeis's role in the New Deal is becoming much clearer as previously closed sources become available. A fine dissertation by Bruce Murphy at the University of Virginia (1978) details the activities of Brandeis and Frankfurter. The economic dilemma faced by the Roosevelt administration is examined in Ellis Wayne Hawley, *The New Deal and the Problem of Monopoly: A Study in Economic Ambivalence* (Princeton, 1966). The best overview of the New Deal is William E. Leuchtenberg, *Franklin D. Roosevelt and the New Deal, 1932–1940* (New York, 1963). For the problems of Jewish refugees see Henry L. Feingold, *The Politics of Rescue: The Roosevelt Administration and the Holocaust* (New Brunswick, 1970).

Index